Strategy for Clarifying Enforcement Needs and Testing Enforcement Measures

This is a three-year strategy designed to address the requirements identified in an assessment of the enforcement challenges and needs within the National Marine Sanctuary System. It provides a framework for the build-up of enforcement capabilities, testing of technologies, and refinement of need. This is not an outline for a comprehensive long-term enforcement program. Rather, it is anticipated that the outcomes from this effort will lead to the development of a comprehensive 10-year enforcement plan. Consequently, this strategy will provide a basis for "learning by doing."

January 2010

National Oceanic and Atmospheric Administration
Office of National Marine Sanctuaries, National Ocean Service
Office of Law Enforcement, National Marine Fisheries Service

For More Information:

Please contact:

Lisa Symons
Office of National Marine Sanctuaries
1305 East-West Highway
Silver Spring, MD 20910
301-713-3125 x275

Stuart Cory
NOAA Office of Law Enforcement
8484 Georgia Ave Suite 415
Silver Spring, MD 20910
301-427-2300 X106

Cover Photo: P/V *Peter Gladding. Photo: Florida Keys National Marine Sanctuary*

TABLE OF CONTENTS

LIST OF TABLES

LIST OF FIGURES

Executive Summary

Through public review of revised site management plans, a 2008 Department of Commerce Office of Inspector General report, and observation, it is clear that the status of enforcement in national marine sanctuaries is woefully inadequate for the mandated level of resource protection of these nationally significant resources. Therefore, this strategy proposes: 1) an increase in overall investment in all sites in the National Marine Sanctuary System, 2) evaluation of the full scope and scale of the enforcement challenges and 3) testing the means to address those issues. It provides a three-year strategy for verifying needs, proposing a core investment in personnel and testing methods for enforcement within the system. Four funding options are included and range from $5 to $25 million. This is neither a comprehensive long-term enforcement requirements document nor an operations plan. However, a program cannot be developed without evaluating enforcement needs and testing potential technologies. It is anticipated that the actions resulting from this strategy will lead to the development of a comprehensive 10-year enforcement requirements plan following the completion of the external evaluation proposed in each option. Consequently, this strategy will provide a basis for "learning by doing."

Enforcement is critical to resource management in marine sanctuaries. Constituents and sanctuary advisory councils consistently identify it as a high priority during sanctuary management plan reviews. Enforcement helps to ensure that our nation's natural and cultural marine resources of national significance are protected. A comprehensive enforcement capability to meet the needs of all sites in the system will take time to develop and require considerable investments in staff, vessels, equipment and technology. This strategy represents a first step towards the development of a comprehensive system-wide enforcement program.

This document outlines major short-term enforcement activities, focused primarily on verifying needs and testing potential enforcement capabilities, to be conducted over the next three years, pending available resources. This three-year strategy summarizes the: current approach to enforcement, status of enforcement activities, and perceived enforcement challenges. The result will be a verified set of enforcement challenges, an assessment of enforcement technologies, and the background knowledge needed for the development of a fact-based, robust 10-year enforcement requirements document for the National Marine Sanctuary System.

There is a wide range of enforcement challenges confronting the ONMS, ranging from spills of oil or other hazardous substances to entanglement of marine mammals in fishing gear, illegal fishing activities, and violations of marine zoning. About 40 challenges were identified in a comprehensive survey of ONMS enforcement issues. Fourteen of these challenges are considered to be a high priority across the entire system based on the number of sites in which they occur. These challenges were identified through surveys completed by ONMS and NOAA Office for Law Enforcement (OLE) staff and form the basis for proposed ONMS enforcement actions over the next three years.

Existing and new enforcement partnerships will need to be enhanced through funding or refined to develop a comprehensive sanctuary enforcement presence. This will include utilizing a combination of resources from NOAA, the U.S. Coast Guard (USCG), other federal resource managers (e.g., the U.S. Department of the Interior), and state resource agencies that currently partner with NOAA.

This report is organized into five sections, focusing on 1) general background and introduction; 2) enforcement approach; 3) status of sanctuary enforcement and existing or potential technologies; 4) enforcement challenges; and 5) options for funding the three-year enforcement strategy. The strategy was developed through a series of steps, engaging staff from across the ONMS as well as OLE, and is based on priority enforcement challenges.

Figure 1. *Map of National Marine Sanctuary System.*

NATIONAL MARINE SANCTUARY SYSTEM

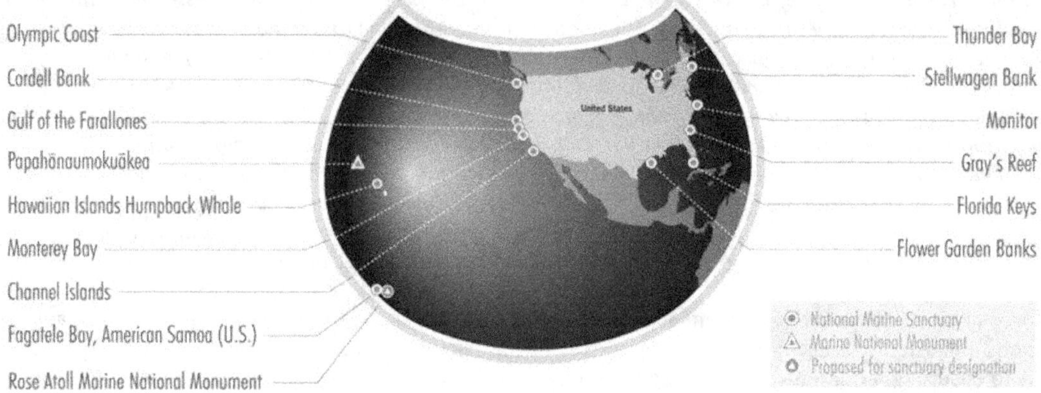

Scale varies in this perspective. Adapted from National Geographic Maps.

I. Introduction

This document is an assessment of current enforcement challenges and needs. It provides a three-year strategy for verifying needs and testing methods for enforcement within the National Marine Sanctuary System. Four funding options are included and range from $3 to $16 million. This is not a comprehensive long-term enforcement requirements document or an operations plan. However, a program cannot be developed without evaluating enforcement needs and testing potential technologies. It is anticipated that the actions resulting from this plan will lead to the development of a comprehensive 10-year enforcement plan. Consequently, this strategy will provide a basis for "learning by doing."

The Office of National Marine Sanctuaries (ONMS) manages a system of 13 national marine sanctuaries and one marine national monument[1]. These sites range in size and complexity, and each site is a unique place requiring special protections. The National Marine Sanctuary System covers more than 150,000 square miles. The costs associated with development, operation, and maintenance of an effective enforcement program are daunting and complicated by the challenges inherent in on-water operations. Consequently, a plan that provides the framework for testing potential methods and building the foundational elements on an enforcement program is needed. This will augment both the existing enforcement efforts and build new capabilities.

Enforcement is a critical resource management tool for marine sanctuaries as it ensures that our nation's natural and cultural marine resources of national significance are protected. Enforcement is consistently identified as a priority in sanctuary management plan reviews. A comprehensive enforcement program at all sites will take time to develop with considerable investments in partnerships, staff, vessels, equipment, and technology. NOAA's Office for Law Enforcement (OLE) leads enforcement efforts in concert with state agencies via cooperative enforcement agreements, and work with the U.S. Coast Guard and other federal agencies authorized to enforce the National Marine Sanctuaries Act and its associated regulations.

There are many enforcement challenges confronting sanctuaries, including balancing resource protection with public use and protecting habitats and living marine resources such as a range of endangered and threatened species, dolphins, seabirds and corals, historical and cultural resources. Over 40 challenges were identified in a comprehensive assessment of sanctuary system enforcement issues. Fourteen challenges are considered to be a priority across the entire system, with many of them occurring frequently. These challenges were identified through surveys with the ONMS and OLE and form the focus of proposed enforcement efforts for the next three years.

Background

The mission of the ONMS is to serve as the trustee for the nation's system of marine protected areas, to conserve, protect, and enhance their biodiversity, ecological integrity and cultural legacy. The ONMS protects 13 national marine sanctuaries and one marine national monument that encompass more than 150,000 square miles of marine and Great Lakes waters[2]. The National Oceanic and Atmospheric Administration (NOAA) has managed national marine sanctuaries since the passage of the Marine Protection, Research, and Sanctuaries Act (now the National Marine Sanctuaries Act) in 1972.

The National Marine Sanctuaries Act (NMSA) authorizes the Secretary of Commerce to designate and manage areas of the marine environment with special national significance due to their conservation, recreational, ecological, historical, scientific, cultural, archeological, educational, or esthetic qualities as national marine sanctuaries. Regulations are promulgated to provide the means for management and protection of these important places. The authority for sanctuary enforcement activities and civil penalties

---

[1] Rose Atoll Marine National Monument was recently added to the system under Executive Order 8337. In addition, Davidson Seamount was added to Monterey Bay National Marine Sanctuary during the management plan review process, increasing the size of the sanctuary by 775 square miles.

is specified in Section 307; Section 312 provides for Natural Resource Damage Assessment authorities. Special agents and enforcement officers of NOAA's OLE have specified authority under NOAA Departmental Organizational Order 25-5 to enforce 37 statutes and numerous treaties for NOAA related to marine conservation and protection, including the NMSA. OLE sworn personnel investigate and make cases for prosecution by NOAA's Office of General Counsel for Enforcement and Litigation (GCEL) or Office of General Counsel for Natural Resources (GCNR) and by referral to the Department of Justice. OLE has the responsibility to oversee cases provided by other law enforcement entities, including those brought by cross-deputized partners or other federal entities.

On June 15, 2006, President George W. Bush made conservation history when he signed Presidential Proclamation 8031, creating the largest fully protected marine conservation area on the planet in the Northwestern Hawaiian Islands. By applying the authority of the Antiquities Act, which gives the president discretion to declare objects or places of scientific or historic interest a national monument, he created the Papahānaumokuākea Marine National Monument (PMNM). On Jan. 6, 2009, President Bush created Rose Atoll Marine National Monument with Presidential Proclamation 8337. The proclamation directs NOAA to incorporate the marine areas of the monument into Fagatele Bay National Marine Sanctuary. As this site is new to the system, it is not included in the threat analysis done by the Fagatele Bay sanctuary personnel, and as such there may be new enforcement issues that will have to be addressed in the operational plan developed once funding is received. Other site expansions, such as the addition of Davidson Seamount to the Monterey Bay sanctuary, will be treated similarly.

A core component of the sanctuary enforcement program is to provide a law enforcement presence to deter and detect violations, deter unlawful activity, educate users and investigate violations. NOAA conducts enforcement operations in sanctuary sites directly through OLE and through cooperative partnerships with other agencies, including the U.S. Coast Guard and U.S. Department of the Interior. Various state marine and wildlife enforcement agencies are also cross deputized by OLE to support sanctuary enforcement.

Enforcement within the sanctuaries began in 1975 at the former Key Largo National Marine Sanctuary with USCG patrols and transitioned to a Cooperative Agreement with the State of Florida in 1980. A similar interagency partnership was established in the early 1980's for Channel Islands National Marine Sanctuary, between the National Marine Sanctuary Program, the National Park Service and the state of California. Additionally, enforcement activities have previously been funded at Hawaiian Islands Humpback Whale National Marine Sanctuary and Stellwagen Bank National Marine Sanctuary. The ONMS has provided funding for an OLE law enforcement officer assigned to the Monterey Bay National Marine Sanctuary since 2003. A specific sanctuary operations plan has been part of NOAA's Joint Enforcement Agreement with the state of Georgia for Gray's Reef National Marine Sanctuary since 2007.

Seven enforcement functions constitute this enforcement program. The functions represent a wide range of activities, including outreach and education, enforcement planning and analysis, investigation and injury assessment, legal mechanisms/processes, management, and asset requirements. See Appendix 3 for more information. Enforcement functions will generally be implemented by personnel from ONMS[3], OLE and other partners.

This strategy document is focused primarily on the enforcement monitoring, patrol and response function. Enforcement monitoring, patrol and response are defined as the field operational aspect of police and regulatory authorities and the implementation of enforcement plans and regulations to protect sanctuary resources. Enforcement monitoring and patrol may include air/sea/land enforcement patrols and near real-time photoreconnaissance, remote sensing techniques, and video monitoring. The function is enhanced and augmented by public and volunteer observations and reporting. The eventual goal for the system is to implement 24/7/365 response capability, site-wide, and have the ability to respond to more than one simultaneous event.

---

[3] ONMS has responsibility for outreach and education, injury assessment and some management asset requirements. (See Appendix 3 for definitions of functions.)

Fourteen priority enforcement challenges are also listed and defined. A challenge was considered a priority if it was identified as a significant challenge by at least three sites. As with any dynamic system, enforcement challenges change over time. During the time it has taken to draft this document, changes have occurred, including the expansion of boundaries and the promulgation of new regulations. These changes were taken into account where possible, but may not be reflected in all instances (such as the inclusion of the new Rose Atoll Marine National Monument). Boundary and system expansions will be addressed in the development of 10-year requirements document and in any necessary operational plans developed for the three-year assessment. The nine technologies considered for enforcement in this three-year strategy are also listed and defined.

This strategy was assembled through a series of steps, summarized in Figure 2. There were considerable interactions with site staff in the development of information about enforcement challenges, frequency of occurrence, and seasonality. In addition, this strategy considers the results of the small boat and aircraft analyses that were conducted independent of this effort. Options for funding the strategy are outlined in Section *VI: Developing the Strategy*. Each option includes a core investment in personnel and various levels of enforcement monitoring technology testing. All of the options meet the initial intent of increasing core resource protection across the National Marine Sanctuary System, analyzing the full scope and scale of the enforcement requirements in each site within the system and determining what the best means to address those issues.

Aircraft flying below the required ceiling in Monterey Bay National Marine Sanctuary. Low overflights harass marine mammals, seabirds and people.

Figure 2. *Process for Development of the Three-Year Enforcement Strategy*

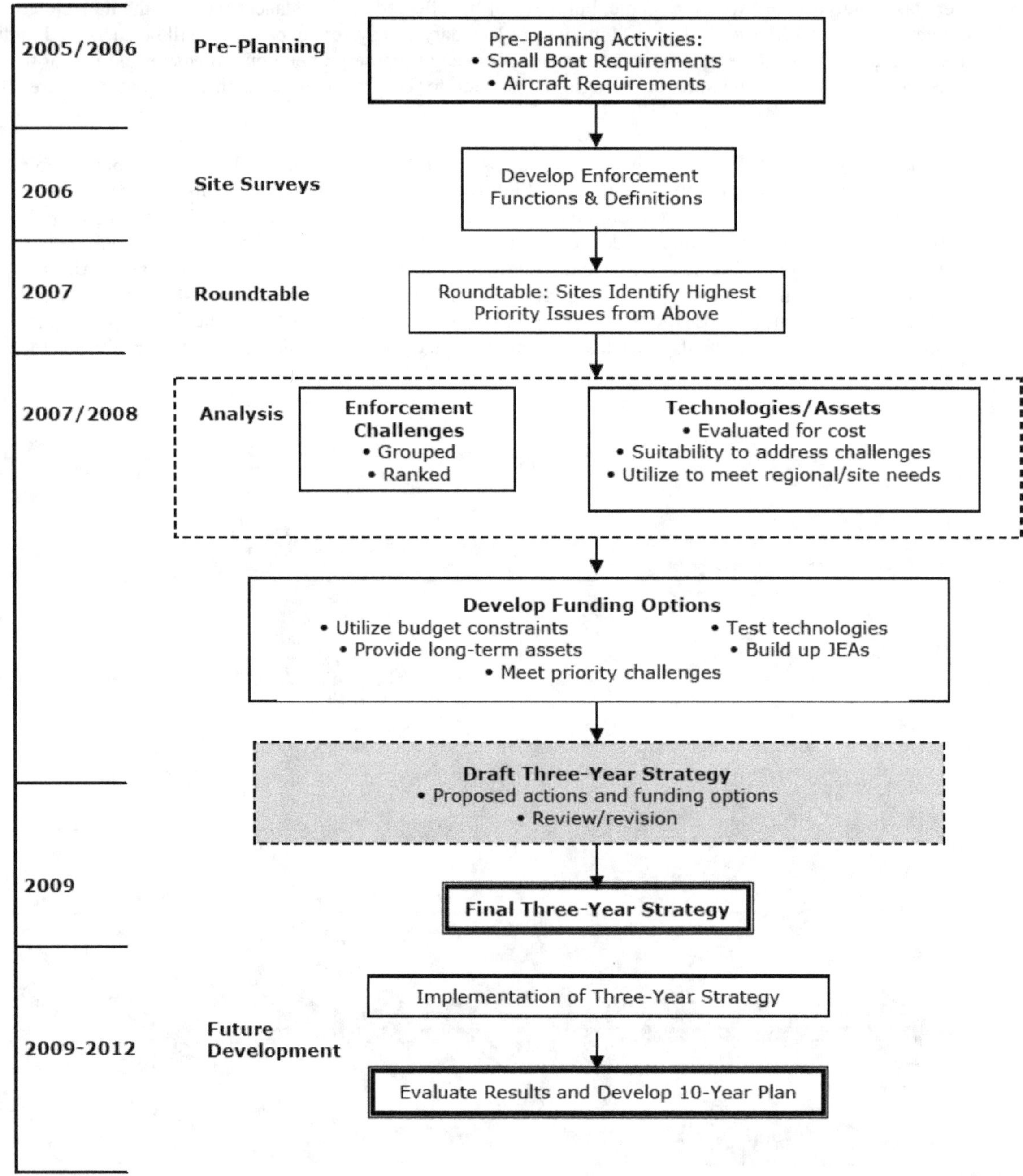

II. Enforcement Approach Phase

Enforcement Philosophy
The sanctuaries' enforcement approach is to prevent and deter injury to sanctuary resources through community-oriented policing and problem solving (COPPS[4]), officer presence, and investigations with the necessary tools to conduct them.

Community-Oriented Policing and Problem Solving (COPPS)
In 1995, the OLE adopted COPPS as a national initiative, designed to empower communities and individuals, to actively participate in their local conservation and management of our valuable living marine resources. OLE firmly believes that effective outreach and the COPPS philosophy are the prime tools for achieving deterrence. OLE's COPPS program is designed to focus on results — not on process and punishment — and the program's foundation rests on education and understanding through teamwork and partnerships. Sanctuaries rely largely on a broad range of education and outreach programs that fit within the concept of COPPS. Previously in the sanctuary system, this has been referred to as "interpretive enforcement," which promotes voluntary compliance through education. The goal of COPPS is to gain the greatest level of compliance through knowledge, understanding and public support of sanctuary goals. COPPS emphasizes informing the public through educational messages and literature about responsible behavior before resources can be adversely impacted. Officers and sanctuary staff talk directly with users and distribute brochures in the field and throughout the community. These encounters allow for informative contact with visitors and local residents while conducting routine enforcement activities. Education and outreach staff and volunteers also provide a critical support element for the COPPS program. For example, the "TeamOCEAN" program, an on-water education and information program at heavily visited sites in Florida Keys and Monterey Bay national marine sanctuaries, is designed to educate users about responsible behavior and sanctuary regulations.

Sanctuaries enforcement is conducted through a fabric of partnerships. Partners include state and federal agencies. Enforcement activities would not be possible within the National Marine Sanctuary System without these arrangements.

Officer Presence
Preventive enforcement is achieved by maintaining a uniformed officer presence sufficient to deter violations. For the sanctuaries, successful enforcement depends on frequent patrols. Water patrols ensure that sanctuary users are familiar with regulations in order to deter willful or inadvertent violations and provide quick response to violations and emergencies. The ONMS relies on its partners, including OLE, the U.S. Coast Guard (USCG), and the states, to provide this capability. Currently this function is performed through cooperative agreements with state agencies, USCG, and in some locations by OLE.

Investigations
OLE is primarily an investigative unit comprised of Special Agents. OLE agents conduct investigations stemming from violations of the NMSA and sanctuary regulations, as well as other federal laws and regulations that occur within sanctuary boundaries. Investigations generally deal with the most egregious and/or habitual violators and can result in positive impact due to heightened awareness and deterrence.

Although there is clearly a need for expansion, COPPS is the well-developed aspect of the sanctuaries' enforcement approach. A uniformed officer presence including tools and technologies is currently the most acute need due to extremely limited resources. Although proficient in its investigative role, additional investigative resources, inclusive of agents and technologies are needed to fulfill OLE's sanctuary

[4] DOJ uses the phrase Community Oriented Policing Services (COPS) Community policing is a philosophy that promotes organizational strategies, which support the systematic use of partnerships and problem-solving techniques, to proactively address the immediate conditions that give rise to public safety issues such as crime, social disorder, and fear of crime. http://www.cops.usdoj.gov/Default.asp?Item=36

enforcement responsibilities.

Enforcement Partners

Sanctuary enforcement cannot be accomplished without state and federal partners. The ONMS does not have the authority to directly enforce regulations for each site. OLE, state agencies via agreements and the U.S. Coast Guard are authorized to enforce sanctuary regulations. In areas of overlapping jurisdiction, the Department of the Interior has authority to enforce NMSA regulations. The NOAA Office of General Counsel provides legal support in conjunction with the Department of Justice.

Congress established the Cooperative Enforcement Program in 2001 to increase the federal, state, and territorial capability for marine resource conservation, endangered species protection, and critical habitat enforcement by providing for deputization through the authority of the Magnuson-Stevens Act to enforce NOAA's statutory authorities. OLE is provided federal funding to establish cooperative work agreements with state resource conservation agencies that perform law enforcement activities for NOAA's statutory mandates. OLE receives authority to carry firearms under the Lacey Act. The Lacey Act also provides the authority for state officers to carry firearms while engaged in federal work.

This program includes two principal components. The cooperative enforcement agreement (CEA) provides the capability for state and U.S. territorial marine conservation law enforcement officers to be cross-deputized to enforce federal law. The joint enforcement agreement (JEA) provides the mechanism to transfer funds to U.S. state and territorial law enforcement agencies. There are active JEAs in almost all of the states that include, or are adjacent to, marine sanctuaries. The exceptions are the state of North Carolina (Monitor National Marine Sanctuary) for state constitutional reasons and Michigan (Thunder Bay National Marine Sanctuary), as Lacey Act doesn't provide statutory authority for historical and cultural resources, only for federally protected fish, plant and wildlife species. JEA funds may be used to secure state enforcement personnel on state-owned vessels conducting on-water enforcement or state personnel as law enforcement officers for NOAA-owned vessels.

While the Coast Guard is a critical partner, it is difficult to quantify the level of support of either on-water or over-water sanctuary enforcement activities because they are generally rolled up into the broader category of living marine resource enforcement or may be a secondary or tertiary activity undertaken during the course of other directed maritime patrols. In addition, Coast Guard presence is valuable for deterrence and increased likelihood of detecting violations. Coast Guard statistics are maintained at a district level, rather than at the more specific level of detail required to determine activities within any given sanctuary, making it difficult to quantify the level of effort and deterrent effect, although it is of critical importance in many of the sites within the system.

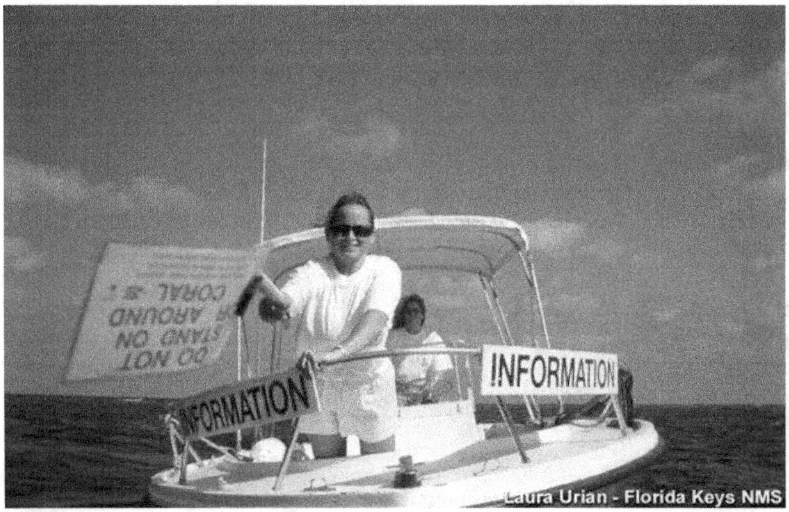

Team OCEAN (Ocean Conservation Education Action Network) is an on-the-water COPPS program aimed at protecting the natural marine resources. It involves stationing trained volunteer teams at heavily visited sites during peak recreational boating seasons.

III. Enforcement Status

The overall enforcement capability within the ONMS is limited (Table 1). Most sites have no staff or are understaffed; a meager capacity given that the system includes 14 marine protected areas, encompassing more than 150,000 square miles of ocean and Great Lakes waters.

Enforcement programs in the sanctuaries are in various stages of development. Most sites have not yet invested significantly in enforcement due to lack of available resources. System-wide, there is an extremely limited capability, given that the total area of all national marine sanctuaries is roughly equivalent in size to the state of California (see Table 3). Chief factors that have hindered development of the ONMS enforcement program include a lack of resources and competing management priorities, expense of enforcement, remoteness and size of sites, differences in regulations between sites, and the complicated nature of state-federal enforcement relationships.

Enforcement in sanctuaries is complex. Enforcement of marine protected areas is resource-intensive, requiring investments in staff, training, vessels, aircraft and technology. Over half of the sites have a significant portion of their holdings in state or territorial waters and about half have either contiguous or overlapping boundaries with other protected areas, such as national wildlife refuges and national parks managed by the Department of the Interior. In addition, this is the only national enforcement program focused solely on marine protected areas. A summary of the current status of enforcement monitoring, patrol, and response assets follows.

Personnel

ONMS does not have an enforcement program coordinator. As part of their duties, two ONMS headquarters resource protection personnel and one OLE headquarters special agent serve as liaisons between the two offices. They meet weekly and periodically with General Counsel for Enforcement and Litigation and with the Coast Guard liaison to OLE.

ONMS funds the equivalent of 17 sworn personnel and two non-sworn personnel, who are state of Florida Fish and Wildlife Conservation Commission (FWCC) employees that work in the Florida Keys. These officers may also be certified as NOAA divers, meet NOAA boat handling requirements, and may be Coast Guard-licensed merchant mariners and work from vessels with both NOAA and Florida FWCC agency logos. OLE has two special agents stationed in the Florida Keys who liaison directly with FWCC and communicate routinely with sanctuary management on enforcement priorities and activities.

One NOAA Law Enforcement Officer funded by ONMS works in the lower and central portions of Monterey Bay National Marine Sanctuary. At the Gray's Reef sanctuary, a site-specific operations plan is included within the JEA between NOAA and the Georgia Department of Natural Resources to provide an on-water enforcement presence. At the Channel Islands sanctuary, Channel Islands National Park, USCG, and California Department of Fish and Game personnel provide some support for violations/incidents. Hawaiian Islands Humpback Whale National Marine Sanctuary has a seasonal OLE presence and a portion of an agent's time to cover the Hawaiian sites. In addition, each site in the system has a designated point of contact from the OLE and from the Coast Guard.

The U.S. Coast Guard (USCG) is present on all U.S. navigable waterways but particularly since 2001, the majority of its resources are focused on maritime domain awareness and/or homeland security. Most of its training and activities for resource protection concentrate on enforcement of fisheries regulations. ONMS should be working more closely with the USCG point of contacts and the appropriate regional Fisheries Training Centers, which have responsibility for training stations, cutters, air stations and sector personnel in sanctuary enforcement, to provide accurate information on sanctuary system resources. Site-specific training with local USCG sectors and districts by ONMS, OLE and GC should augment this. In general, USCG personnel are first responders for dealing with general boater safety, marine emergencies and when dealing with oil spill and hazardous materials incidents[5]. Sites have been much more proactive in engaging local USCG assets to increase attention to sanctuary issues. USCG capacity for this enforcement is currently limited due to other priorities; however, both agencies have an interest in efficient, productive use of assets to support sanctuary management.

Additionally, ONMS resource protection personnel, utilized in the event of a spill, grounding, or other incident impacting sanctuary resources, are present at seven sanctuaries (Channel Islands, Florida Keys, Flower Garden Banks, Gulf of the Farallones, Hawaiian Islands Humpback Whale, Monterey Bay and Olympic Coast) and the Papahānaumokuākea Marine National Monument. These personnel provide injury assessments for use in either civil penalty or natural resource damage assessment cases. They are also critical in providing on-site guidance during response actions such as salvage that may cause additional injury to sanctuary resources. In addition, there are three historical and cultural resource personnel that are available to sites across the system.

Vessels, Aircraft, and Patrol Vehicles

Over the next three years, the program will refine the operational requirements and limitations of a broad range of conventional capital assets necessary to build an enforcement capability. Currently, there are limited enforcement assets in the system. Only one of the 14 sites has dedicated enforcement vessels (Florida Keys). Those assets are currently owned and operated by ONMS and supported out of the ONMS Small Boat Program. Currently there is no regular NOAA aircraft presence for enforcement at any sanctuary, although ONMS was able to fund some time for enforcement in FY2009 on a NOAA Twin Otter although USCG does fly over most sites on a periodic basis and ONMS has been working with regional airstations to develop new patrol guides that address sanctuary regulations. Table 1 summarizes current enforcement assets in the sanctuary system. In other sites such as Gray's Reef, state or federal partners have vessels that are also reflected in Table 1 (Note: USCG assets are not reflected in Table 1). Operation of new dedicated enforcement vessels presumes either state or federal law enforcement officers or agents for that purpose. Those personnel will either be from NOAA OLE, or other state or federal partners. While direct supervision of those personnel must be done through established chains of command for the respective agencies, frequent regular coordination with ONMS is essential to ensure that resource protection priorities are being met and that emerging challenges can be addressed.

This strategy builds on previous ONMS Vessel and Aircraft Requirement documents and the categories of vessels and aircraft they identified. The initial assumptions for this document are that nearshore sites will require the minimum of Type II vessels for safe operations, and for offshore sites or sites with limited operational conditions either a Type III or possibly a Small Research Vessel (SRV) will be the minimum for enforcement monitoring, patrol and response. Discussions about the viability of multi-purposing sanctuary vessels to address both enforcement and other resource management priorities such as research and education have focused on safety of non-law enforcement personnel when law enforcement staff are not onboard. It is possible that removable signage could address part of this issue, allowing fo the most efficient use of a single asset. Multi-purposing of aircraft does not have the same perceived risks.

- *Fixed-Wing Aircraft* include light twin-prop, medium turboprop, and large turboprop planes. Their range varies from 500 to 2,500 nautical miles, cruising speeds from 150-170 knots, and a flying duration from five to 10 hours. Crew would include two-three flight and two-four mission staff.
- *Helicopters* have a range of 300 nautical miles, a cruising speed up to 110 knots, and a flying duration of up to 2.5 hours.
- *Patrol Vehicles* are required for all officers. In many instances, they must be capable of trailering a Type I or Type II vessel.
- *Small Research Vessels* (SRV) are greater than 80 feet in length, have a range of 1,700 nautical miles, a cruising speed of 30 knots, and a seven-day duration. These vessels possess an extended overnight capability, wet labs, and other facilities on board.

---

[5] While USCG may be first called in FKNMS, they frequently hand over response to the Florida Fish and Wildlife Commission officers.

- *Type I Vessels* are less than 29 feet in length, have a range of 150 to 200 nautical miles, a cruising speed of 15 knots, and eight- to 10-hour duration.
- *Type II Vessels* are 30 to 49 feet in length, have a range of up to 300 nautical miles, a cruising speed of 20 knots, and an eight- to 10-hour duration.
- *Type III Vessels* are greater than 50 feet in length, have a range of up to 500 nautical miles, a cruising speed of 35 knots, and a four- to five-day duration.

Enforcement Monitoring Technologies

In and of themselves, enforcement technologies cannot supplant an on-water or active law enforcement presence, nor do they negate the need for follow-up and investigation.

Although advanced technologies are being utilized to a limited extent for enforcement monitoring in sanctuaries, there is tremendous potential for expansion. Currently, a small low altitude, short endurance unmanned aerial system is being tested in the Papahānaumokuākea Marine National Monument for identification of marine debris. Automatic Identification Systems (AIS) and Vessel Tracking Systems (VTS), which alert port authorities and the USCG regarding the movement and disposition of vessels, are being utilized in Olympic Coast and Stellwagen Bank national marine sanctuaries to ascertain adherence to vessel traffic separation measures. While AIS and VTS are active for most major ports, the program is not actively using that information. The USCG issued a Federal Register Notice of Proposed Rulemaking to adjust AIS carriage requirements down to vessels of 65 feet or greater earlier this year. Vessel monitoring systems (VMS) are being used for several active fisheries and are monitored by the OLE for adherence with federal fishery regulations. All vessels within the monument must have VMS. High-frequency radar is being used in coastal waters near San Francisco to provide general oceanographic observations. Low-frequency radar is frequently being used for vessels and aircraft. Some of the available technologies are listed below, others such as the use of Forward Looking Infrared Radar (FLIR) on aircraft or other assets are not specifically discussed as separate technologies, but could be an asset deployed from either vessels or aircraft.

Technology	Definition
Acoustic Buoys	Buoys (active buoys) provide the capability to detect activities or incursions into areas or distribute a signal (passive buoys) for preventive purposes (e.g., alerting vessels to stay out of "Areas To Be Avoided"). Passive systems, such as the RACON beacon system currently in the Florida Keys sanctuary, is mounted on navigational structures along the reef tract, emit distinct signals that warn ships they are nearing the coral reef in time for them to make appropriate corrections.
Automatic Identification System (AIS)	An FM frequency-based system monitored by the USCG used by ships and traffic monitoring systems for vessel collision avoidance and to identify and locate vessels. The system provides a ship name, radio call sign, master's name, course, position and speed to other nearby ships or traffic monitoring systems. It is currently required for electronic submission of notice of arrival and departure. USCG is in a rulemaking process to decrease the vessel size requirements for use of AIS for port entry in the United States.
Autonomous Unmanned Systems (AUS)	AUS include unmanned surface and subsurface vessels that could serve two purposes: 1) reconnaissance and enforcement monitoring, and 2) scientific data collection and research. There is no significant AUS activity in the ONMS at the current time.
Electronic Intelligence (ELINT)	Electronic Signals Intelligence refers to the gathering of information by use of electronic sensors. ELINT can be used to detect ships and aircraft by their radar and other electromagnetic radiation. ELINT can be collected from ground stations, aircraft, or by satellite. ELINT data is often highly classified information, but in some instances both unclassified and classified data streams

are available. *For this document we are only addressing unclassified data.*

RADAR	Radar (high-frequency) is used to measure ocean surface currents and is being explored for oil spill tracking or (low-frequency) to determine if vessels or aircraft are present in selected areas. HF Radar is currently used in sanctuaries off the California coast in the event of oil spills and low-frequency radar is used to identify vessels operating in areas that should be avoided (i.e., no entry zones).
Satellites	Satellites can be used to monitor marine traffic, increasingly in real-time. Imagery can also be used for determining user counts or for assessing pollution events. Commercial systems do this currently. Commercial satellite companies do not place their imagery into the public domain and do not sell their imagery except through licenses. This data tends to be expensive.
Unmanned Aerial Systems (UAS)	Includes unmanned aerial platforms capable of operating at altitudes from approximately 2,000 to 25,000 feet and endurances from two to 25 hours. These devices could be used for remote enforcement monitoring/natural resource monitoring activities. A low-altitude, short-endurance UAS is currently being tested at the Papahānaumokuākea Marine National Monument. Currently, FAA guidelines place significant limitations on use of this technology in domestic airspace.
Vessel Monitoring Systems (VMS)	This is a satellite-based system used in specific commercial fisheries to allow for the monitoring of position, time and duration at position, course and speed of fishing vessels. There are over 5,000 VMS-equipped fishing vessels monitored by OLE in the U.S. This is expected to increase significantly with the addition of vessels in the newly designated Pacific Marine Monuments.
Vessel Tracking System (VTS)	There are two main types of VTS, surveilled and non-surveilled. Surveilled systems consist of one or more land-based sensors (i.e. radar, AIS and closed circuit television sites), which output their signals to a central location where operators monitor and manage vessel traffic movement. Non-surveilled systems consist of one or more required reporting points for ships to report their identity, course, speed, and other data. They encompass a wide range of techniques and capabilities aimed at preventing vessel collisions, rammings and groundings in the harbor, harbor approach and inland waterway phase of navigation. They are also designed to expedite ship movements, increase transportation system efficiency and improve all-weather operating capability. VHF-FM communications network providing active monitoring and navigational advice for vessels in particularly confined and busy waterways. Transiting vessels make position reports to a vessel traffic center by radiotelephone and are in turn provided with accurate, complete, and timely navigational safety information. The addition of a network of radars, AIS, and closed-circuit television cameras for enforcement monitoring and computer-assisted tracking, similar to that used in air traffic control, allows the VTS to play a more significant role in marine traffic management, thereby decreasing vessel congestion, critical encounter situations and the probability of a marine casualty resulting in environmental damage. The Coast Guard operates 12 Vessel Traffic Centers (VTC), four of which are near sanctuaries: Puget Sound, Seattle, San Francisco, Los Angeles/Long Beach, and Houston-Galveston.

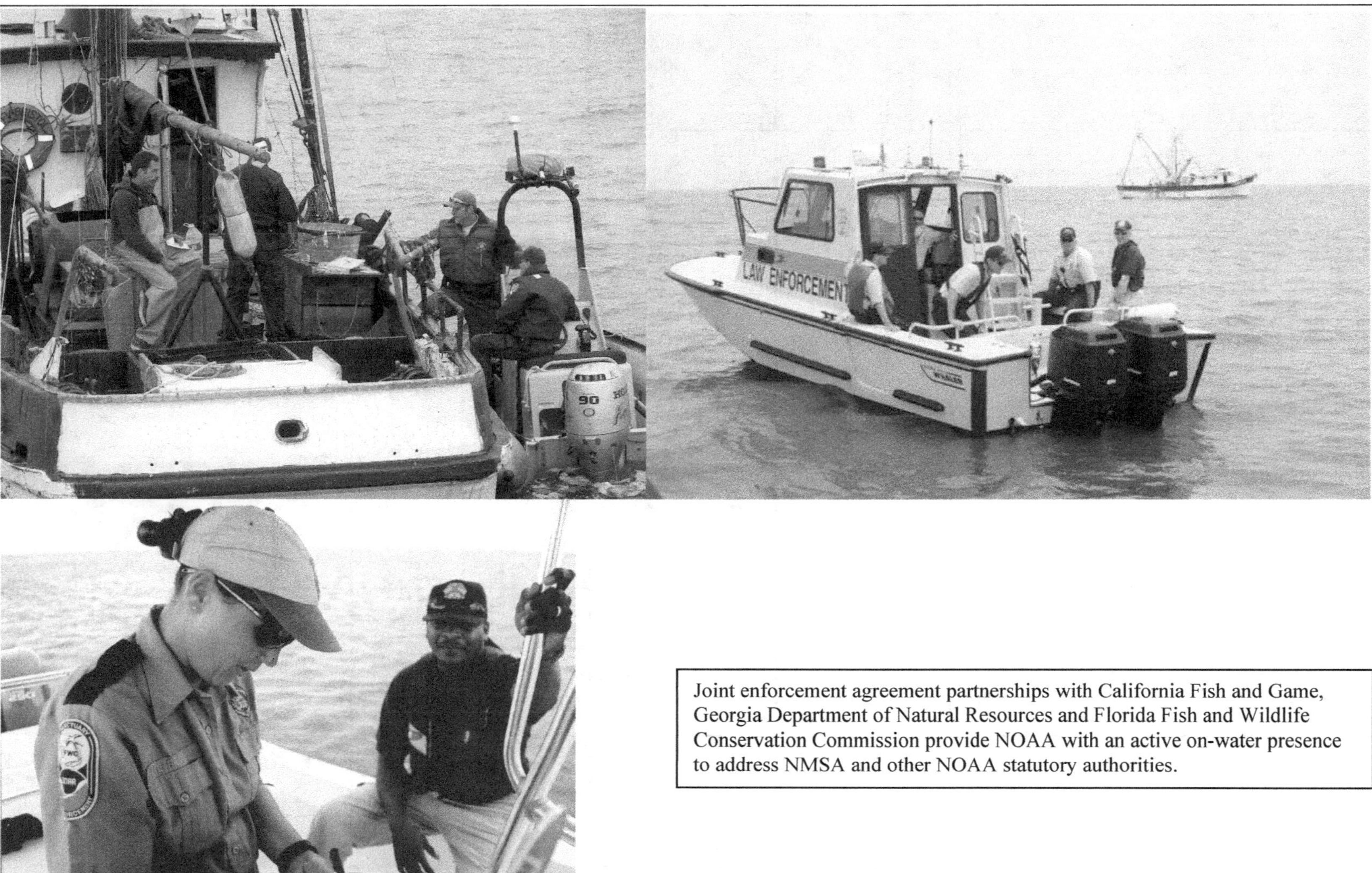

Joint enforcement agreement partnerships with California Fish and Game, Georgia Department of Natural Resources and Florida Fish and Wildlife Conservation Commission provide NOAA with an active on-water presence to address NMSA and other NOAA statutory authorities.

Table 1. *Status of Enforcement Assets (USCG Assets are reflected in Appendix 4)*

	NE/GL			SE/GOM			WC					PAC				
	M	SB	TB	FK	FG	GR	CI	CB	GF	MB	OC	FB	HI	PM	Total	Notes
Staff (number FTE)																
Enforcement staff (FTE)				17						1					18	
Enforcement Hours (JEA) (Vessel Hours)						90									90	Decreased from 180 vessel hours due to increased fuel costs.
Vessels (number)																
Type 1 (<29')				4						1					5	
Type II (30-49')				5		(2-3)									5 (7-8)	Vessels in parens are Georgia DNR.
Type III (>50')				1											1	
Small Research Vessel (>80')							-	-	-	-	-					SRVx in testing within WCR region in FY08, 09.
Aircraft (hours)																
Light Twin Prop				-												FWCC makes their aircraft available on intermittant basis.
Medium Turboprop							-	-	-	-	-					Active Testing of NOAA Twin Otter in CINMS, MBNMS, GFNMS for enforcement overflights, included night observations. NOAA Twin Otter to be deployed to California in November 2008.
Large Turboprop					-									-		USCG currently uses a C130 for intermittant overflights.
Helicopter	-	-	-	-	-	-	-	-	-	-	-	-	-	-		Currently in use by USCG in most operating areas, principally for search and rescue purposes.
Enforcement Monitoring Technology (units)																
Umanned Aerial System Low-Altitude Short Endurance (UAS/LASE)							1						1	1	1	Tested UAS/LASE at HIHWNMS, CINMS (in-shore) and PMNN. PMNM owns UAS/LASE.
Umanned Aerial System Medium-Altitude Medium Endurance (UAS/MAME)																NOAA assessing capabilities primarily for climate research.
Umanned Aerial System High-Altitude Long Endurance (UAS/HALE)																NOAA assessing capabilities primarily for climate research.
Autonomous Unmanned Systems (UAS)																Potential testing of system at PMNM.
Automatic Information System (AIS)		1									1				2	System utilized in large ports for commerical vessels. Sanctuary specific feeds for OCNMS Area to be Avoided and SBNMS Vessel Traffic Zones (Right Whale Avoidance).
Vessel Monitoring Systems (VMS)														1	1	Using VMS at PNMS to check for fishing vessels.
Radar - Low Frequency																Potential six month deployment by Naval Research Lab prototype in Tortugas National Park to observe Tortugas Ecological Reserves in FKNMS.
Radar - High Frequency								1	1	1					3	Currently being used in Northern Management Area of MBNMS and GFNMS to observe oceanographic currents. Some value for pollution trajectories.
Electronic Intelligence																Not being utilized in ONMS. Potential six month deployment by Naval Research Laboratory in Dry Tortugas National Park to observe Tortugas Ecological Reserves in FKNMS.
Active and Passive Buoys				1											1	Passive systems used in the FKNMS. Potential test of Naval Research Laboratory prototypes at TBNMS, MNMS and GRNMS.
Satellites	-	-	-	-	-	1	-	-	-	-	-	-	-	-	1	User assessments possible for all sites. Issues associated with access to either commercial or previously classified data. GRNMS has used satellites for user counts, Being considered for other sites, particularly in PMNM.
Enforcement Agreements																
Cooperative Enforcement Program		MA		FL	TX LA	GA	CA	CA	CA	CA	WA	AS	HI	HI	9	There are active CEA/JEA in all but two of the states. GRNMS has a site-specific operations plan. CINMS, MBNMS and FKNMS have a seperate MOUs that will be transitioned to site-specific operations plan in the JEA.
NOAA Office of Law Enforcement	1	1	1	1	1	1	1	1	1	1	1	1	1	1	14	Additional point of contact at headquarters for a total of 15 points of contact.

IV. Enforcement Challenges

This section summarizes the priority challenges, their potential spatial extent, and frequency of occurrence. Enforcement challenges were identified, characterized and assessed to build this three-year programmatic strategy. Data about challenges were gathered via a comprehensive survey, including frequency of occurrence and area of impact. ONMS site personnel and their respective OLE points of contact answered the survey jointly. Data were subsequently organized and analyzed. An additional round of site-specific prioritization of enforcement challenges by sanctuary representatives took place during an enforcement roundtable session at an ONMS Leadership Team meeting in September 2007.

A systematic assessment of all enforcement challenges resulted in the identification of the 14 most important challenges across the system. The challenges were identified through a survey and follow-up roundtable.

A system-wide assessment was conducted with sanctuary staff in 2006 to determine enforcement challenges and their frequency of occurrence (number of events per year) at ONMS sites. Sanctuary representatives identified priority challenges for each site with a system-wide list of over 40 different issues. Additional analysis of this data identified all challenges that occurred in three or more sites, resulting in a narrowed list of 14 system-wide enforcement challenges. In order to provide the best potential system-wide assessment, all 14 sites in the system are included in the analysis.

Enforcement Challenges

Challenge	Definition/Description
Commercial Fishing	Commercial fishing means fishing in which the fish are harvested to enter commerce. Charter and headboat "for hire" fishing may be considered recreational. Commercial fishing can be a common activity within sanctuaries and may be subject to specific regulations regarding location, gear, season, catch limits, etc.
Cruise Ship Discharges	Cruise ships are commercial passenger vessels with a carrying capacity of 250 or more passengers, and sleeping facilities for each passenger. Cruise ships can produce large volumes of waste, on a larger scale than other vessels of similar size. Cruise ship discharges include any release, disposal, spilling, leaking, pumping, etc.
Entanglement/Marine Debris—Biological	Marine species, including whales, turtles, seabirds, and sessile organisms such as coral, can become entangled or ensnared in floating marine debris such as derelict fishing gear, nets and plastics. In addition, entanglement can occur from active fishing gear such as longlines, trap gear and gill nets.
Entanglement/Marine Debris—Maritime Heritage	Submerged cultural and archeological resources are susceptible to becoming entangled in floating marine debris such as derelict fishing gear or nets. This can result in damage to historic shipwrecks or other irreplaceable sanctuary resources. In addition, entanglement can occur from active fishing gear such as trawl nets and anchors.
Fishing/Fishing Gear Violations	Fishing in a prohibited manner, in a prohibited area (reserve, protected or restricted area), with prohibited gear or through the retention of illegal species or sizes can negatively impact sanctuary resources. This applies to both recreational and commercial fishing activities.
Illegal Salvage Operations/Looting	Any destructive activities that impact the structural and cultural integrity of historic marine resources. Cultural and archeological resources are protected under the NMSA, the Antiquities Preservation Act, the National Historic

	Preservation Act and others.
Large Commercial Vessel Traffic	Large commercial vessels may carry large volume cargo and have significant bunker fuels on board. Commercial vessels or merchant ships can be divided into three broad categories: cargo ships, passenger ships, and special-purpose ships.
Marine Life Disturbance by Aircraft	Aircraft operating at low altitudes can disturb marine mammals, turtles and seabirds, disrupting their resting, mating or rearing of young, feeding, or other normal activities.
Marine Mammal Injury/Harm and Permits/Takings	Marine mammals are protected in national marine sanctuaries by the Marine Mammal Protection Act (MMPA) and, in some cases, the Endangered Species Act. Enforcement is important to protect them from being harassed, hunted or killed without the required permits under the MMPA.
Recreational Vessel Activities	Vessels (e.g., kayaks, personal watercraft, pleasure craft) used for recreational rather than commercial purposes can pose a range of enforcement challenges including marine life harassment, illegal discharges, and user conflicts.
Marine Zone	A marine zone is defined as a discrete area within a national marine sanctuary that is subject to different regulations than the rest of the sanctuary. A marine zone can be established to better manage resources and activities and does not inherently mean a no-take zone. The official federal definition of a marine protected area (MPA) is: "any area of the marine environment that has been reserved by federal, state, tribal, territorial, or local laws or regulations to provide lasting protection for part or all of the natural and cultural resources therein." — Executive Order 13158 (May 2000). In practice, MPAs are defined areas where natural and/or cultural resources are given greater protection than the surrounding waters. In the U.S., MPAs span a range of habitats including the open ocean, coastal areas, inter-tidal zones, estuaries, and the Great Lakes. They also vary widely in purpose, legal authorities, agencies, management approaches, level of protection, and restrictions on human use. Sanctuaries are considered MPAs and may have additional zoning established within them to address specific resource protection and management issues.
Illegal Discharge/ Spills of Unknown Origin	Illegal discharges and marine spills of oil, hazardous substances, or other materials into sanctuary waters or those that may enter and injure sanctuary resources are of concern.
Traffic Routing/ Anchoring Incidents	Any system of traffic routing measures aimed to reduce the risk of casualties; it includes traffic separation schemes, two-way routes, recommended tracks, areas to be avoided (ATBAs), no-anchoring areas, inshore traffic zones, precautionary areas including Particularly Sensitive Sea Areas. Anchoring incidents (in a no-anchoring area in particular) can cause injury to sanctuary resources such as coral, seagrass or historical and cultural resources.
Vessel Groundings	Vessels that run aground on shore or in shallow waters can do major injury to sanctuary resources; for example, destroying coral reefs, seagrass flats or scattering debris across tide pools.

The Papahānaumokuākea Marine National Monument (PMNM) is undertaking a separate enforcement threat assessment that may change the characterizations in this document of enforcement challenges within the monument. Jurisdiction for this site is complicated with co-management responsibilities shared between NOAA, the Department of the Interior and the state of Hawaii. PMNM is the largest site in the system, encompassing 139,797 square miles—and because of its vast size and remote location, enforcement approaches must be specially tailored. In addition, that the PMNM has a different statutory authority as it was designated under the Antiquities Act. The information reflected here is the best estimate of resource managers as to what the challenges are for the site.

Table 2 lists the system-wide priority enforcement challenges. Those affecting the most sites include illegal discharges/spills of unknown origin, fishing/fishing gear violations, traffic routing/anchoring incidents, entanglement/marine debris—biological, and large commercial vessel traffic. The sites with the largest number of these priority issues include Gulf of the Farallones, Monterey Bay, and Florida Keys national marine sanctuaries, and the PMNM.

Table 2. *Priority Enforcement Challenges by Site.*

		Northeast/Great Lakes			Southeast/Gulf of Mexico			West Coast					Pacific		
Priority Challenge	Total #	M	SB	TB	FG	FK	GR	CB	CI	GF	MB	OC	FB	HI	PM
Traffic Routing/Anchoring Incidents	11	•	•	•	•		•		•	•	•	•		•	•
Fishing/Fishing Gear Violations	8				•	•	•	•		•	•	•	•		
Spills of Unknown Origin	8	•	•		•				•	•	•	•			•
Entanglement/Marine Debris-Biological	7					•	•			•	•	•	•	•	
Large Commercial Vessel Traffic	7		•			•		•		•	•			•	•
Recreational Vessel Traffic	7			•	•	•				•	•			•	•
Commercial Fishing	6	•	•			•				•	•				•
Cruise Ship Discharges	5					•		•		•	•	•			
Entanglement/Marine Debris-Maritime Heritage	5	•	•	•								•			•
Illegal Salvage Ops./Looting	5	•	•	•		•									•
Marine Mammal Injury/Harm and Permits/Takings	5						•			•	•			•	•
SPA or Zone	5					•			•	•	•				•
Vessel Groundings	5					•			•	•	•				•
Marine Life Disturbance by Aircraft	4								•	•	•	•			

This table shows priority enforcement issues identified by three or more sites in the NMSS. Sites are grouped by region. While this provides an overview of shared enforcement challenges within the system it does not reflect the full range of issues at individual sites. A site may have issues that are of more significance locally that aren't among the top 14 found nation-wide.

Table 3 provides a comparison between priority challenges and the potential spatial extent (sum of area for sanctuaries listing that as a priority). Consequently, the area affected by enforcement challenges may be overstated. Enforcement methods must account for the importance of a challenge's spatial extent. This table helps to portray those challenges that have a large spatial "footprint." Due to its vast size, PMNM is not included in Table 3. It encompasses 139,797 square miles—substantially more than Monterey Bay NMS (5,319 square miles), the next largest site. Enforcement methods used in the PMNM must be able to address priority challenges that extend over a large area. In addition, due to the fact that PMNM was created under the Antiquities Act and is co-managed with the state of Hawaii and the U.S. Department of Interior, special regulation and enforcement provisions exist.

Table 4 summarizes the frequency of occurrence of priority challenges. The Monterey Bay, Gulf of the Farallones and Florida Keys sanctuaries are the only sites with priority challenges that occur more than 50 times per year (although many sites had challenges among the larger total list of 40 that occur more than 50 times per year.) All three sites list commercial fishing and recreational vessel traffic as priorities occurring at least 50 times per year. These challenges should be strong candidates for testing methods within this three-year strategy. Fishing, fishing gear violations, marine zones, groundings, and overflight violations also occur frequently at the sites and make excellent candidates for testing enforcement methods.

Table 3. *Summary of Priority Enforcement Challenges, by Number, Site, and Total Area.*

		Area (thousand square miles)													Area (1000 sq mi)*	% Total Area*
Enforcement Challenge	Total #	4	5	6	7	8	9	10	11	12	13	14	15	16		
Traffic Routing/Anchoring Incidents	11														14 9	78
Spills of Unknown Origin	8														15 1	79
Entanglement/Marine Debris-Biological	8														13 1	69
Fishing/Fishing Gear Violations	7														15 9	83
Large Commercial Vessel Traffic	7														13 1	74
Recreational Vessel Traffic	7														11 0	69
Commercial Fishing	6														10 0	64
Cruise Ship Discharges	5														12 8	78
Entanglement/Marine Debris-Maritime Heritage	5														4 5	24
Illegal Salvage Ops /Looting	5														5 1	27
Marine Mammal Injury/Harm and Permits/Takings	5														6 7	47
SPA or Zone	5														11 9	67
Vessel Groundings	5														11 9	67
Marine Life Disturbance by Aircraft	4														11 3	63

*The PMNM is not included in the table due to its vast size (139,797mi2)

Table 4. *Intensity and Frequency of Priority Enforcement Challenges by Site.*

		Northeast/Great Lakes			Southeast/Gulf of Mexico			West Coast					Pacific		
Priority Challenge	Total #	M	SB	TB	FG	FK	GR	CB	CI	GF	MB	OC	FB	HI	PM
Traffic Routing/Anchoring Incidents	11														
Fishing/Fishing Gear Violations	8														
Spills of Unknown Origin	8														
Entanglement/Marine Debris-Biological	7														
Large Commercial Vessel Traffic	7														
Recreational Vessel Traffic	7														
Commercial Fishing	6														
Cruise Ship Discharges	5														
Entanglement/Marine Debris-Mar.Heritage	5														
Illegal Salvage Operations/Looting	5														
Marine Mammal Injury/Harm//Takings	5														
SPA or Zone	5														
Vessel Groundings	5														
Marine Life Disturbance by Aircraft	4														

Intensity (# occurrences per year)

>50   10 to 50   <10

V. Developing the Strategy

This section presents four potential strategies to test and develop elements of a comprehensive enforcement program for the sanctuary system, while providing for initial improvements in resource protection through deterrence, compliance and enforcement. The options range in cost from $5.4 to $34.7 million over a three-year period, as illustrated in Figure 3.

The three-year strategy consists of several key components: enhanced staffing, vessel and aircraft support; leveraging of partnerships including maximizing use of joint enforcement agreements with states; and testing and evaluation of all enforcement assets.

The overarching objective is to provide a range of options that would allow for the testing of different enforcement capabilities at ONMS sites. Four enforcement options are proposed to test and evaluate enforcement strategies. The higher cost alternatives reflect increases in both labor and technology testing and usage. All ONMS sites with their unique opportunities and logistical differences were considered and ideally all should have some enforcement effort occur within their sites over the three-year period. The potential for sharing of technology, staff, or assets across regions or sites or with enforcement partners was taken into account. Budget constraints were utilized to develop the options to meet priority enforcement challenges, test technologies for program-wide use, determine long-term enforcement coordination needs, provide long-term assets, test conventional versus high tech options, and build up JEAs.

Figure 3. *Comparison of Option Totals and Category Expenditures*

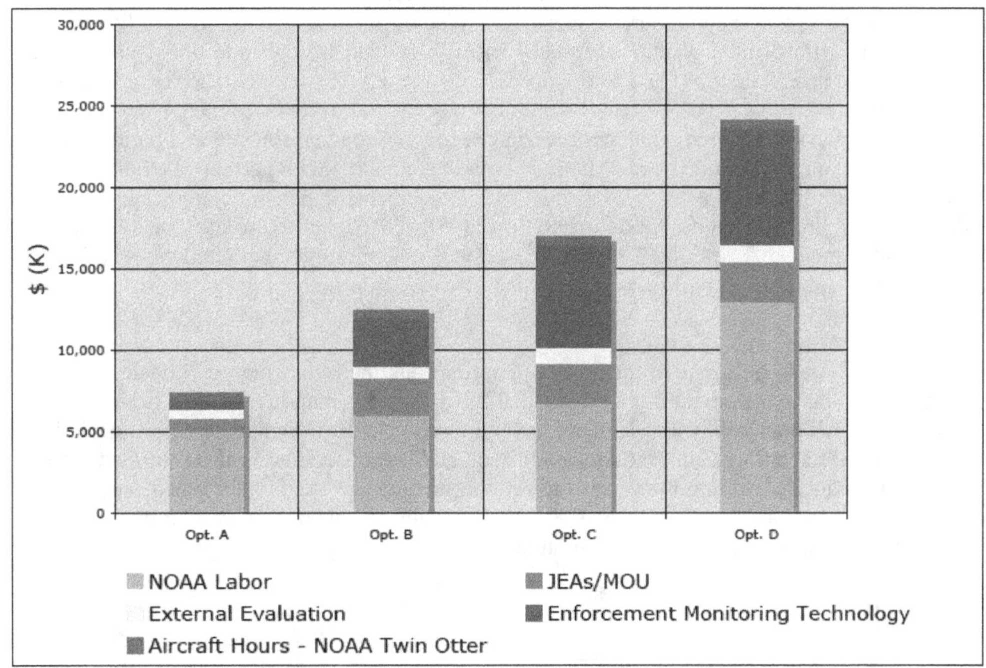

A number of assumptions are factored into these options. The unmanned aerial systems (UAS) and autonomous unmanned systems (AUS) may be dependent on U.S. Coast Guard cutter support once the USCG Research and Development Center gets clearance for the use of AUSs within the fleet and determines which types are the most effective. The UAS technology is also complicated by current flight restrictions by the Federal Aviation Administration that currently preclude the use of UAS in most coastal waters. Also, although JEAs are a cost-effective method for providing a law enforcement presence on the water, differing state requirements may result in differing enforcement capabilities between states.

The ONMS enforcement program's highest priority is to hire a national enforcement coordinator and then two regional enforcement coordinators. This non-sworn position will be responsible for coordinating with enforcement partners to implement the actions outlined, evaluating outcomes and alternatives and developing the subsequent, more comprehensive 10-year enforcement requirements plan.

The NOAA OLE's highest priority for the sanctuary enforcement mission is to establish and provide direct, ongoing and substantive enforcement services in all sanctuary sites in accordance with the assessed needs of each site within the system. The OLE provision of sanctuary enforcement services is a clear and compelling component of the overall successful NOAA management of sanctuary resources. The OLE will direct existing personnel and hire the appropriate new enforcement officers to jointly implement the strategy for clarifying enforcement needs and testing enforcement measures as funds become available.

Another critical component is the further utilization of existing data streams for enforcement monitoring, in this case, the use of AIS/VTS and VMS data, where available. The ongoing evaluation of the three-year strategy as it unfolds will be critical in the analysis necessary to develop an effective 10-year enforcement requirements document. NOAA proposes that this evaluation be supported by an external and impartial contract. An OLE agent will be needed to support this process part-time, in addition to the ONMS enforcement coordinator and the OLE points of contact for each site or region. This will allow the agent to be more effective with time dedicated to the evaluation process, above and beyond the existing coordination with the points of contact.

What Will It Take?

Sustaining current levels of enforcement within ONMS sites and the further development of a comprehensive enforcement program will require additional resources. The preliminary assessment of enforcement challenges shows that the number, frequency and type of potential violations greatly outweighs the current resources. The enforcement system is currently insufficient and requires additional staff, vessels, vehicles and technology to meet its current and future needs. Existing asset investments for enforcement are not adequately maintained nor replaced as the life cycle end of a particular asset is reached. New methods and technologies will need to be explored and managers will need to leverage resources and partnerships. Key components of an expanded program need to include broad agreements with partners/agencies, utilization of existing capabilities such as AIS/VTS and VMS, investments in personnel and capital assets over an extended period of time, personnel training, and development of "job aids" to provide on-water guides for enforcement personnel. The ONMS and OLE must verify the enforcement challenges and field-test potential enforcement solutions to build an effective and efficient enforcement program.

How Will We Get There?

Upon receipt of additional funding for one of the proposed options, an operations plan will be developed using this strategy as a guidance document but ensuring that the operations plan is reflective of the current enforcement challenges. This plan will be implemented over a three-year time frame and will result in an improved understanding of the enforcement monitoring, patrol, and response requirements for the ONMS, as well as critically important insight into the various techniques that can be used to address these key enforcement challenges. A comprehensive 10-year enforcement requirements document will be developed after an analysis of the lessons learned during the initial three-year phase.

Table 5. *Summary of Funding Options*

Sanctuary Enforcement Strategies- Funding Options				Funding Option ($K)												Summary			
				Option A			OptionB			Option C			Option D			Total Cost ($K/3yr)			
Asset(s)		Site(s)	Challenge(s)	Year 1	Year 2	Year 3	Year 1	Year 2	Year 3	Year 1	Year 2	Year 3	Year 1	Year 2	Year 3	Opt. A	Opt. B	Opt. C	Opt. D
1. Staff																			
1.1	ONMS Enforcement Coordinator (salary+budget)	HQ	All	200	200	200	200	200	200	200	200	200	200	200	200	600	600	600	600
1 2	ONMS Regional Enf. Coordinators (salary)	(NEGL/ SER) WCR	All										300	300	300				900
1 3	External Evaluation of Assessment Strategy	HQ	All	100	100	300	250	250	250	300	300	400	300	300	400	500	750	1,000	1,000
1.4	NOAA EOs - ($350K/yr1, $160K/yr2+)	ALL regions	All	2,100	960	960	2,800	1,280	1,280	2,800	1,280	1,280	5,600	2,560	2,560	4,020	5,360	5,360	10,720
1 5	NOAA OLE - Enforcement Evaluator	HQ		125	125	125	250	250	250	250	250	250	250	250	250	375	750	750	750
1.6	JEAs Boat Hours Boat Hours Personnel/Boat/Aircraft Hours Personnel/Boat/Aircraft Hours Personnel/Boat/Aircraft Hours Personnel/Boat/Aircraft Hours MOU with NPS	GR CA* SB FK OC FG GF/MB	All	40 250	40 250	40 250	40 325 50 250 50 50	40 325 50 250 50 50	40 350 50 250 50 50	40 325 50 250 50 50 50	40 325 50 250 50 50 50	40 350 50 250 50 50 50	40 325 50 250 50 50 50	40 325 50 250 50 50 50	40 350 50 250 50 50 50	870	2,295	2,445	2,445
2. Enforcement Monitoring Technology and Support																			
2.1	Satellite Technology Acquisition - Imagery	All	Most	100	100	100	100	100	100	350	350	350	400	400	400	300	300	1,050	1,200
2.2	Acoustic Buoys - NRL Deployment and Support	TB/SB/PM	Anchoring Incidents, Illegal Salvage				750	400	400	1,000	750	750	1,000	750	750		1,550	2,500	2,500
2.3	Sonobuoys Deploy in GR; redeploy in CB in year 1 5	GR/CB	Zoning, Large Commercial Vessel Traffic, Recreational							300	265	265	300	265	265			830	830
2.4	EL NT (6 month NRL project) Technology Acquisition - ELINT	FK	Fishing Gear, Lg Comm Vessel Traffic, Rec	250			250			250			250			250	250	250	250
2.5	UAS (LALE) Training - UAS Technology Acquisition , O&M Vessel Support (NOAA/USCG)	CA*, PMNM, FGB	Most				100 125 50	100 125 50	100 125 50	200 250 100	200 250 100	200 250 100	200 250 100	200 250 100	200 250 100		300 375 150	600 750 300	600 750 300
2.6	AUS Technology Acquisition, O&M	PMNM											250	250	250				750
2.7	AIS/VTS Enforcement - USCG Available, requires engagement w/ OLE personnel	H HW, OC, CA*, SB, FK	Large Commercial Vessel Traffic													NC	NC	NC	NC
2 8	VMS - Software update/licensing fees for direct ONMS access to data; Available on indirect basis via OLE	ALL	Selected Fishing and Fishing Gear Issues, SPA/Zoning	50			50			50			50			50	50	50	50
3. Aircraft and Vessels																			
3.1	Aircraft Hours - NOAA Twin Otter (350 hrs/yr at $150K)	WCR	Most	150	150	150	150	150	150	150	150	150	150	150	150	450	450	450	450
3 2	Type III Vessel Acquisition ($1.5M each)	NW	All																
3 3	Vessel O&M ($250K/yr) & Engineer ($100K/yr)	NW	All																
SUBTOTAL				**3.365**	**1.925**	**2.125**	**5.840**	**3.670**	**3.695**	**7.015**	**4.910**	**5.035**	**10.415**	**6.790**	**6.915**	**7.415**	**13.180**	**16.935**	**24.095**

*CA = CI, MB, GF, CB

Figure 4 provides an illustration of the relative investments in each of the expenditure categories. All of the options show increased labor costs in year one, reflecting initial expenses for the hiring and training of federal law enforcement officers. The options build to a relatively robust funding scenario that not only provides a significant increase in resource protection within the system, but also provides a three-year assessment of the resource threats enabling the development of a 10-year funding requirements plan.

Figure 4. *Comparisons between Options for Differing Expenditure Categories*

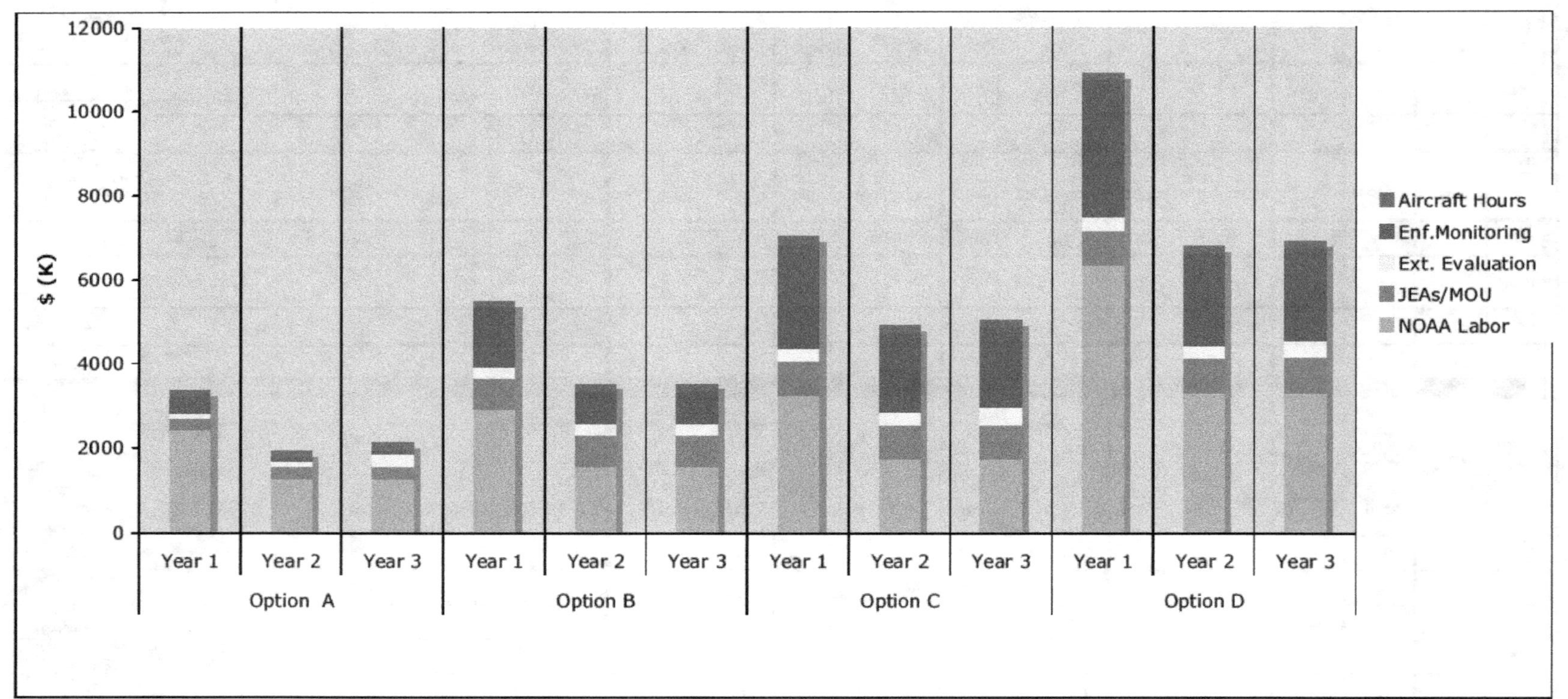

Funding Option A: ($7.415 million)

This $7.4million option emphasizes staff, leveraging technologies and aircraft. This is a "bare-bones" option that provides only basic enforcement needs, focusing on enhancing NOAA's presence as a deterrent.

Aircraft. This option calls for an investment of $450K over the three-year period. It represents approximately 350 hours of medium fixed-wing aircraft time. It is anticipated that it would be applied primarily for both routine patrol and high-intensity events within the four sites in California.

Evaluation Contract. This option calls for $500K to evaluate and analyze the effectiveness of various enforcement assets to address challenges through a series of partner surveys and interviews. This will be critical for eventual development the 10-year requirements document.

Joint Enforcement Agreements. About $870K in funding would be applied towards joint enforcement agreements to enhance on-water enforcement presence at selected sanctuaries. JEAs represent a relatively quick and cost-effective method to provide on-water enforcement services at sanctuaries. At many sites, the staff and supporting requirements (i.e., patrol car, vessel, etc.) already exist.

Staff. This option would result in the funding of three federal staff. It would include the hiring of the ONMS enforcement coordinator and six NOAA Enforcement Officers (EOs). Two are recommended for the West Coast Region for California and Washington, one in the Pacific Islands Region and, three for the P/V *Peter Gladding* in the Florida Keys sanctuary. First-year expenditures for EOs are significantly more than outyears, as they include training and equipment. It would result in six and one-half NOAA full time equivalent (FTEs)(an ONMS enforcement coordinator, six NOAA EOs and half of an agent's time for oversight of the evaluation work).

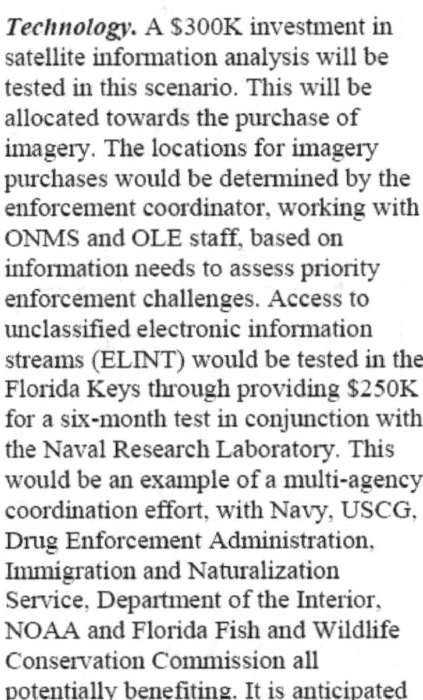

Technology. A $300K investment in satellite information analysis will be tested in this scenario. This will be allocated towards the purchase of imagery. The locations for imagery purchases would be determined by the enforcement coordinator, working with ONMS and OLE staff, based on information needs to assess priority enforcement challenges. Access to unclassified electronic information streams (ELINT) would be tested in the Florida Keys through providing $250K for a six-month test in conjunction with the Naval Research Laboratory. This would be an example of a multi-agency coordination effort, with Navy, USCG, Drug Enforcement Administration, Immigration and Naturalization Service, Department of the Interior, NOAA and Florida Fish and Wildlife Conservation Commission all potentially benefiting. It is anticipated that ELINT would help to address fishing/fishing gear violations and anchoring of large commercial vessel traffic, and recreational vessel traffic in the no-anchoring area. Satellite imagery would also be purchased and analyzed at selected sites to help determine more about usage patterns, adherence with vessel traffic schemes, and no-entry areas. AIS/VTS and VMS technologies can be deployed by OLE and ONMS with minimal investment as the infrastructure already exists for five of the sites near large ports. A $50K

Figure 5. *Labor Category Comparisons*

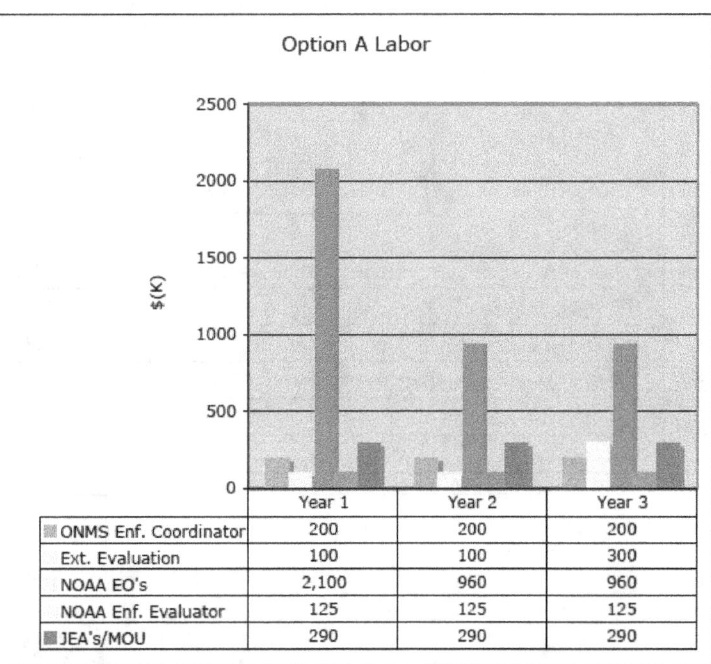

	Year 1	Year 2	Year 3
ONMS Enf. Coordinator	200	200	200
Ext. Evaluation	100	100	300
NOAA EO's	2,100	960	960
NOAA Enf. Evaluator	125	125	125
JEA's/MOU	290	290	290

investment in VMS software and training will provide information regarding adherence to zoning, gear restrictions and non-NMSA authorities.

Vessels. This option does not include the acquisition of vessels.

Figure 6. *Yearly summary of proposed expenditures for Option A.*

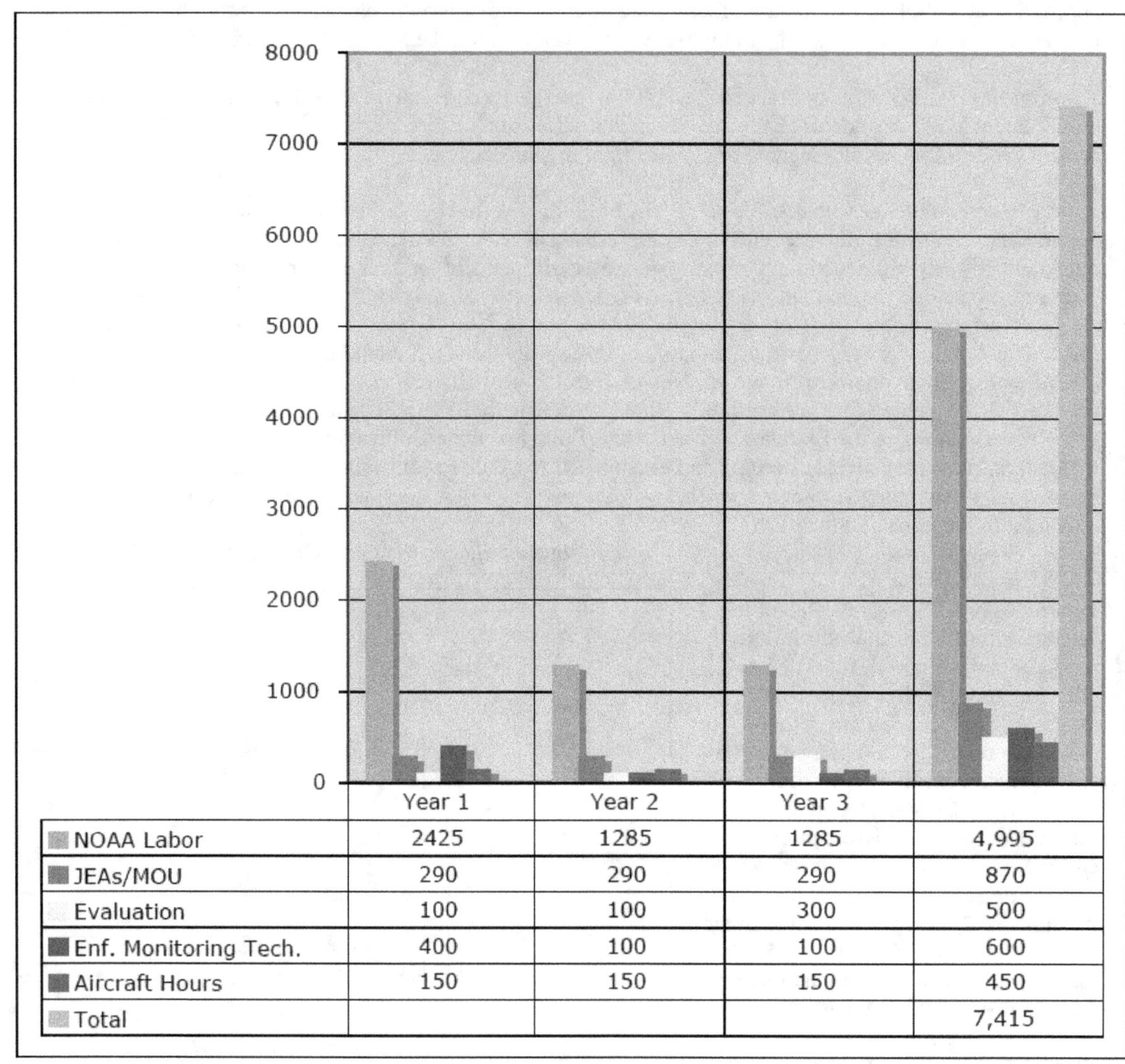

	Year 1	Year 2	Year 3	
NOAA Labor	2425	1285	1285	4,995
JEAs/MOU	290	290	290	870
Evaluation	100	100	300	500
Enf. Monitoring Tech.	400	100	100	600
Aircraft Hours	150	150	150	450
Total				7,415

Funding Option B: ($12,510 million)

This $12.5 million option emphasizes a mix between providing additional staffing, testing some enforcement monitoring technologies, including acoustic buoys and an unmanned aerial system. This option would provide for the testing of four technologies at multiple sites.

Aircraft. This option calls for an investment of $450K over the three-year period. It represents approximately 350 hours of medium fixed-wing aircraft time. It is anticipated that it would be applied primarily for both routine patrol and high-intensity events within the four sites in California.

Evaluation Contract. This option calls for $750K to evaluate and analyze the effectiveness of various enforcement assets to address challenges through a series of partner surveys and interviews. This will be critical for eventual development the 10-year requirements document.

Joint Enforcement Agreements. $2.3M would be applied towards joint enforcement agreements to enhance the on-water enforcement presence. JEAs represent a relatively quick and cost-effective method for providing an on-water enforcement presence. At many sites, the staff and supporting requirements (i.e., patrol car, vessel, etc.) already exist. A $150K investment in the regional partnership with the National Park Service in the San Francisco Bay area will provide additional support for Monterey Bay and Gulf of the Farallones national marine sanctuaries.

Staff. An ONMS enforcement coordinator would be hired to implement and evaluate the activities outlined in this strategy. Funding for seven NOAA law enforcement officers, and a full-time agent to assist with oversight of the evaluation process is provided in this option. One EO is recommended for the Pacific Islands Region (PIR), Pacific Islands Divisions (PID), two for the West Coast Region (WCR), South West Division, and Northwest Division (/SWD/NWD) one for the NorthEast Great Lakes Region (NEGL) and North East Division (NED) and three for the P/V *Peter Gladding* in Florida Keys NMS. First-year expenditures for EOs are significantly more than outyears, as they include training and equipment.

Technology. This option builds on Option A with the addition of acoustic buoy and UAS support. Four technologies would be included within this option. Acoustic buoys would be tested at the Thunder Bay and Stellwagen Bank sanctuaries to address vessel traffic/anchoring incidents and illegal salvage operations/looting. This would involve coordination with the U.S. Naval Research Lab. This array would provide information regarding boater activity in the area and could be calibrated to notify law enforcement when illegal anchoring is taking place. The challenges addressed by this technology include zoning, large commercial vessel traffic, and recreational vessel impacts.

Vessels. There is no acquisition of vessels in this option.

Figure 7. *Labor Category Comparisons*

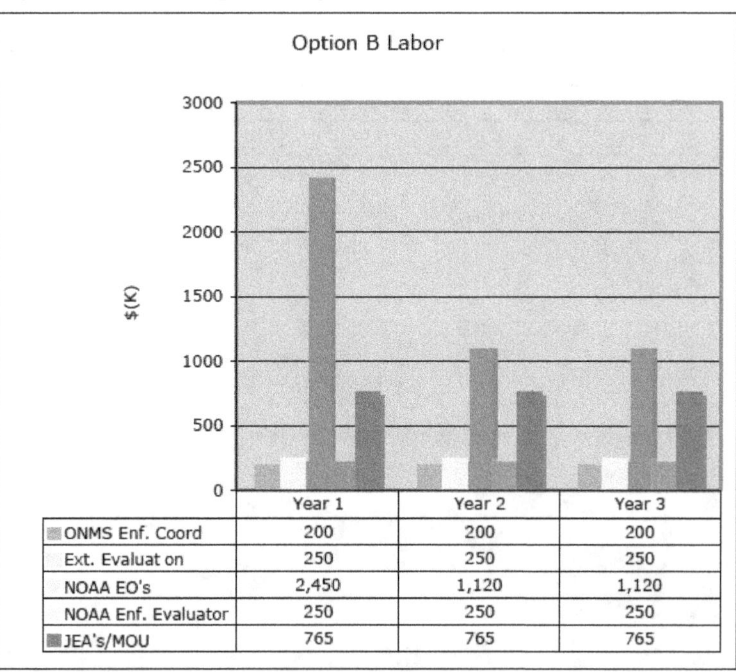

	Year 1	Year 2	Year 3
ONMS Enf. Coord	200	200	200
Ext. Evaluat on	250	250	250
NOAA EO's	2,450	1,120	1,120
NOAA Enf. Evaluator	250	250	250
JEA's/MOU	765	765	765

Figure 8. *Yearly summary of proposed expenditures for Option B.*

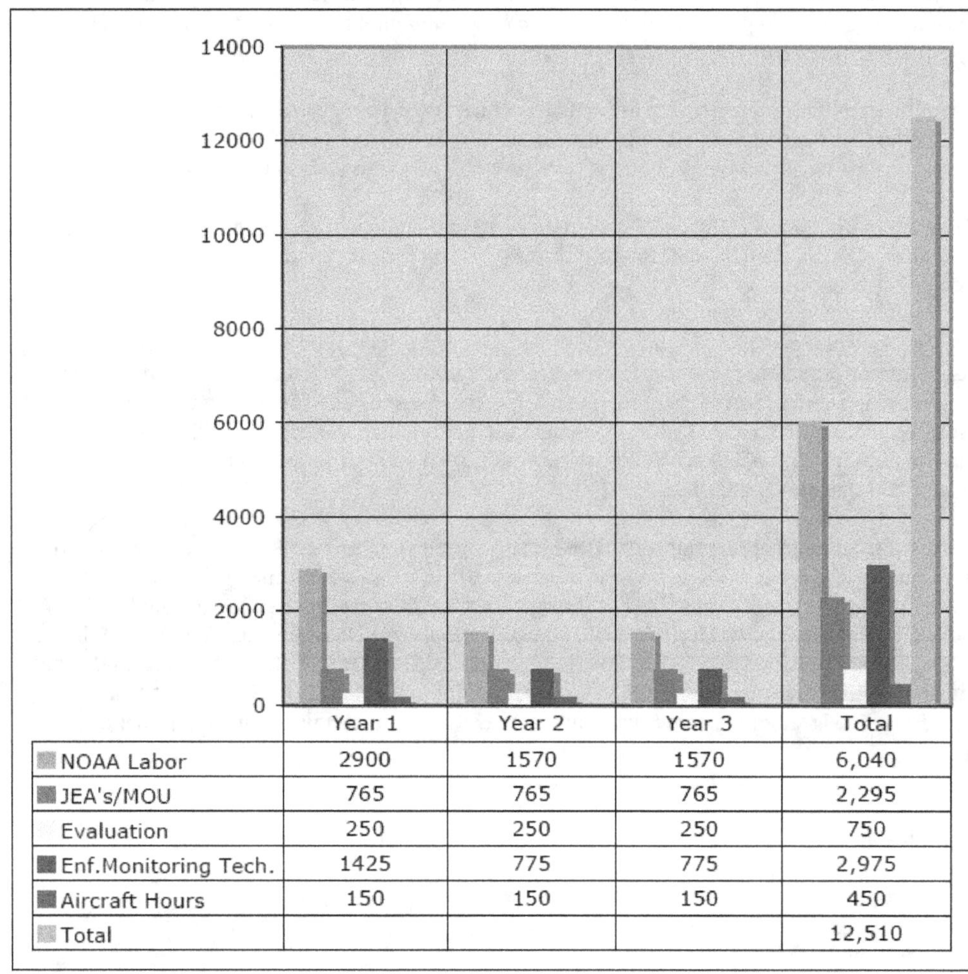

	Year 1	Year 2	Year 3	Total
NOAA Labor	2900	1570	1570	6,040
JEA's/MOU	765	765	765	2,295
Evaluation	250	250	250	750
Enf.Monitoring Tech.	1425	775	775	2,975
Aircraft Hours	150	150	150	450
Total				12,510

Funding Option C: ($16,960 million)

This $16.9 million expands on Option B, with the provision of additional staffing and more enforcement monitoring technology testing.

Aircraft. This option calls for an investment of $450K over the three-year period. It represents approximately 350 hours of medium fixed-wing aircraft time. It is anticipated that it would be applied primarily for both routine patrol and high-intensity events within the four sites in California.

Evaluation Contract. This option calls for $1M to evaluate and analyze the effectiveness of various enforcement assets to address challenges through a series of partner surveys and interviews. This will be critical for eventual development the 10-year requirements document.

Joint Enforcement Agreements. About $2.4M in funding would be applied towards joint enforcement agreements to enhance the on-water enforcement presence at selected sanctuaries. JEAs represent a relatively quick and cost-effective method for providing an on-water enforcement presence. At many sites, the staff and supporting requirements (i.e., patrol car, vessel, etc.) already exist. A $150K investment in the regional partnership with the National Park Service in the San Francisco Bay area will provide additional support for the Monterey Bay and Gulf of the Farallones sanctuaries.

Staff. This option would result in the funding of 11 federal staff. It would include the hiring of the ONMS enforcement coordinator, nine NOAA EOs, and a full-time agent to assist with oversight of the evaluation process. Two EOs are recommended for PIR/PID, two for the WCR/SWD/NWD, two for the NEGL/NED and three for the P/V *Peter Gladding* in the Florida Keys Sanctuary. First-year expenditures for EOs are significantly more than outyears, as they include training and equipment.

Technology. This option provides for the same technology as in Option B, except it also includes a significant funding increase ($1.05 million total) for satellite technology and $830K for buoy technologies. The purchase of a commercially available system (SEAWATCH) would be deployed at Gray's Reef and Cordell Bank national marine sanctuaries. This array would provide information regarding boater activity in the area and could be calibrated to notify law enforcement when illegal anchoring is taking place. It would also provide an effective means of monitoring the pending new research-only area within the Gray's Reef sanctuary. The challenges addressed by this technology include zoning, large commercial vessel traffic, and recreational vessel impacts. Unmanned Aerial Systems (UAS) technology testing would include two years of training prior to acquisition of aircraft.

Vessels. No vessels would be purchased under this option.

Figure 9. *Labor Category Comparisons*

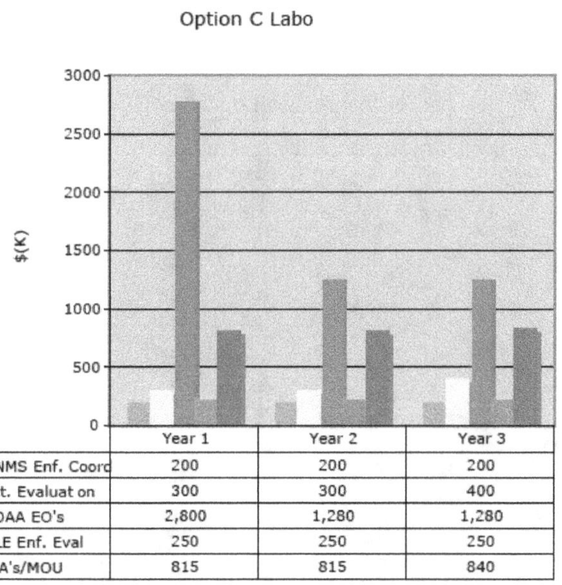

Option C Labo

$(K)

	Year 1	Year 2	Year 3
ONMS Enf. Coord	200	200	200
Ext. Evaluat on	300	300	400
NOAA EO's	2,800	1,280	1,280
OLE Enf. Eval	250	250	250
JEA's/MOU	815	815	840

Figure 10. *Yearly summary of proposed expenditures for Option C.*

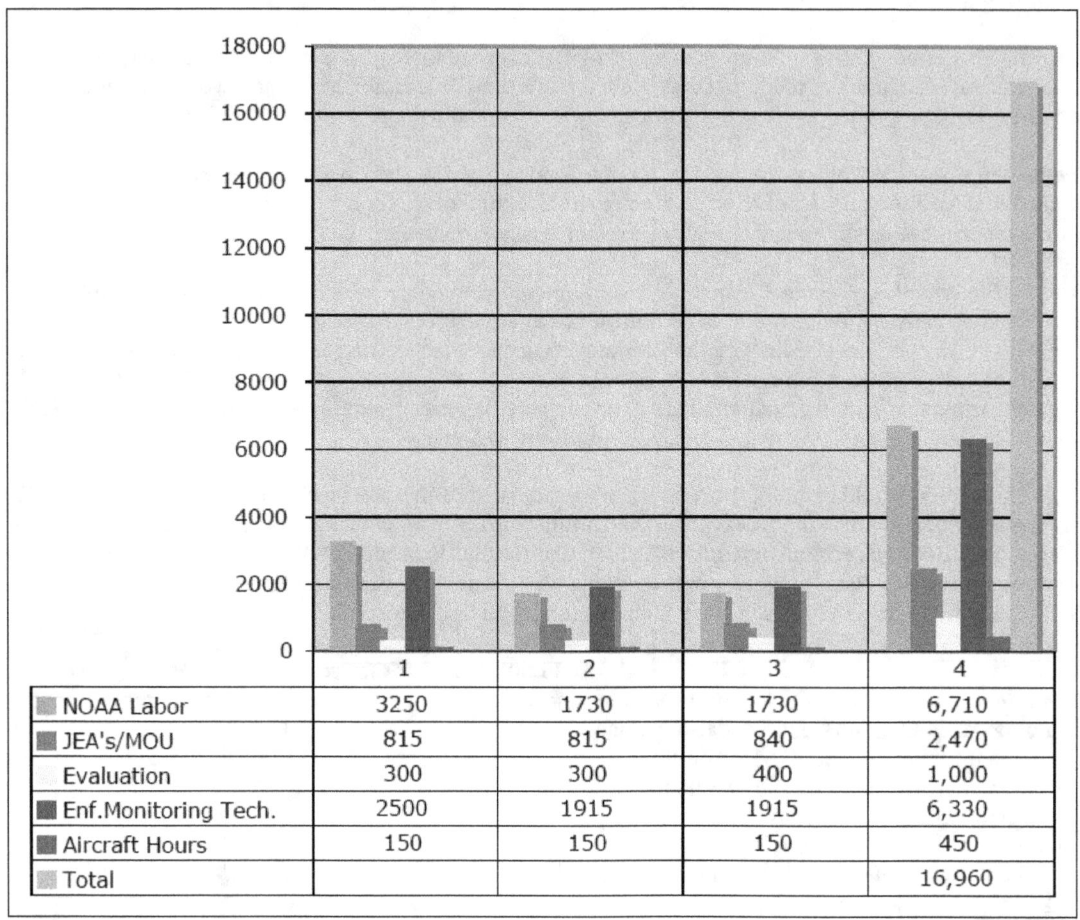

	1	2	3	4
NOAA Labor	3250	1730	1730	6,710
JEA's/MOU	815	815	840	2,470
Evaluation	300	300	400	1,000
Enf.Monitoring Tech.	2500	1915	1915	6,330
Aircraft Hours	150	150	150	450
Total				16,960

Funding Option D: ($24,620 million)

This $24.6 million option is the most robust funding proposal provided in this strategy document. It includes a significant investment in personnel and the opportunity to evaluate a full range of enforcement monitoring technologies.

Aircraft. This option calls for an investment of $450K over the three-year period. It represents approximately 350 hours of medium fixed-wing aircraft time. It is anticipated that it would be applied primarily for both routine patrol and high-intensity events within the four sites in California.

Evaluation Contract. This option calls for $1M to evaluate and analyze the effectiveness of various enforcement assets to address challenges through a series of partner surveys and interviews. This will be critical for eventual development the 10-year requirements document.

Joint Enforcement Agreements. About $2.4M in funding would be applied towards joint enforcement agreements to enhance the on-water enforcement presence at selected sanctuaries on new NOAA law enforcement vessels. JEAs represent a relatively quick and cost-effective method for providing an on-water enforcement presence. In many sites, the staff and supporting requirements (i.e., patrol car, vessel, etc.) already exist. A $150K investment in the regional partnership with the National Park Service in the San Francisco Bay area will provide additional support for Monterey and Gulf of the Farallones.

Staff. This option would result in the funding of twenty federal staff. It would include the hiring of the ONMS enforcement coordinator, two ONMS regional enforcement coordinators, 16 NOAA EOs and a full-time agent to assist with oversight of the evaluation process is provided in this option. Two EOs are recommended for PIR/PID, six for the WCR/SWD/NWD, three for the NEGL/NED, three for the P/V *Peter Gladding* in the Florida Keys sanctuary and two for the SEGOM/SED. First-year expenditures for EOs are significantly more than outyears, as they include training and equipment.

Figure 11. *Labor Category Comparisons*

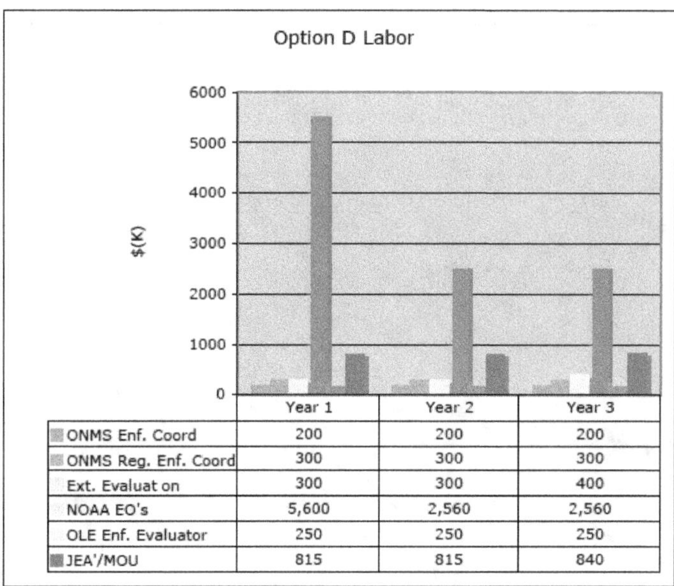

	Year 1	Year 2	Year 3
ONMS Enf. Coord	200	200	200
ONMS Reg. Enf. Coord	300	300	300
Ext. Evaluat on	300	300	400
NOAA EO's	5,600	2,560	2,560
OLE Enf. Evaluator	250	250	250
JEA'/MOU	815	815	840

Technology. $7.23 million would be invested in technology in Option D with small increases in satellite data investments and the use of an AUS. This option would allow for testing all of the technologies identified. In several instances, technologies can be tested without NOAA having to fully invest in acquisition.

Vessels. No vessels would be purchased under this option.

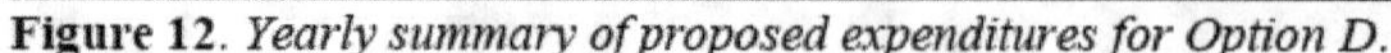

Figure 12. *Yearly summary of proposed expenditures for Option D.*

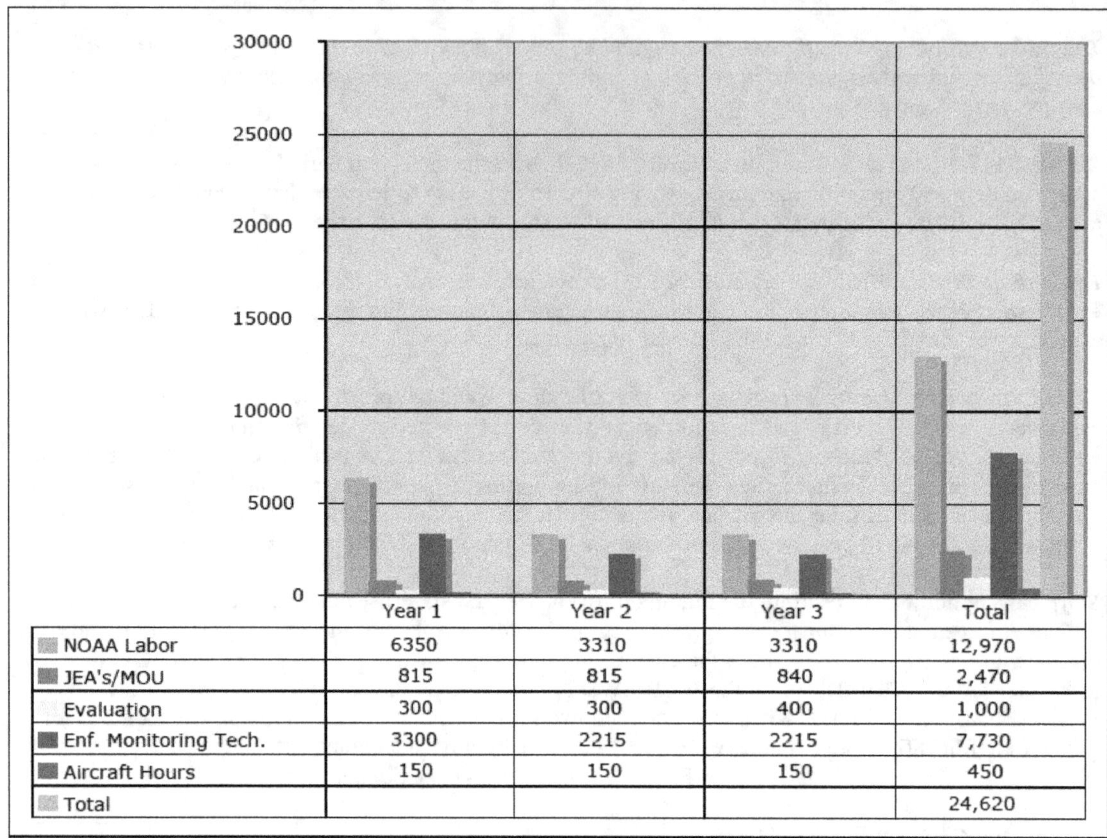

	Year 1	Year 2	Year 3	Total
NOAA Labor	6350	3310	3310	12,970
JEA's/MOU	815	815	840	2,470
Evaluation	300	300	400	1,000
Enf. Monitoring Tech.	3300	2215	2215	7,730
Aircraft Hours	150	150	150	450
Total				24,620

VI. Summary

Compliance with sanctuary regulations, achieved through an active enforcement capability, is an essential element of the ONMS. It has been consistently identified as a high priority need in most if not all sanctuary management plan reviews. Enforcement helps to ensure that our nation's natural and cultural marine resources of national significance are protected. A comprehensive ONMS enforcement program will take years and considerable investments in staff, vessels, equipment and technology. This plan represents a first step towards the development of a comprehensive system-wide ONMS enforcement program.

This document outlines major short-term enforcement activities, focused primarily on testing potential enforcement technologies, to be taken over the next three years. This three-year plan: 1) identifies the enforcement needs of the ONMS as they are currently known; 2) describes the methods and technologies available to meet those needs, and; 3) identifies possible sites for testing of potential technologies. This information, in addition to a rigorous analysis of current enforcement assets and capabilities and a cost-benefit analysis of all the capabilities are necessary to move the system forward. The end result of this process will be a verified set of ONMS enforcement needs, a new set of technologies for use in meeting those needs and the data, experience and knowledge to serve as the basis for the development of a fact-based, robust 10-year enforcement requirements document.

There are a wide range of enforcement challenges confronting the ONMS, ranging from illegal discharges, spills of oil, petroleum products or other hazardous substances to entanglement of marine mammals in fishing gear and marine debris. About 40 issues were identified in a comprehensive assessment of ONMS enforcement challenges. Fourteen challenges are considered to be a high priority across the entire system, with varying frequency and intensity.

In order for NOAA to meet the growing expectations of the public as we revise management plans and sanctuary sites become more mature, we must step up to the next set of management requirements and institute an efficient, cost-effective enforcement program that can be adaptive to the changing needs of the sanctuary system as it grows and matures. The analysis that takes place during this process will be fundamental to building such a capability and capacity to protect America's underwater treasures.

VII. Appendices

Appendix 1. Summary of Challenges by Site

Pacific Region

Fagetele Bay National Marine Sanctuary. Fagetele Bay has two priority challenges, fishing/fishing gear violations and entanglement/marine debris-biological. A limited number of enforcement challenges occur at the site less than 10 times per year. These include commercial fishing and gear violations, recreational vessel traffic, groundings, anchoring incidents, and entanglement/marine debris. None of the challenges except hurricanes have a seasonal component, but fishing, entanglements, and search and rescue support result in nighttime enforcement requirements. There are no shared or contiguous boundaries, although the site is in territorial waters. There are two reserves/protected areas/zones with differing regulations than the rest of the site.

Hawaiian Islands Humpback Whale National Marine Sanctuary. The Hawaiian Islands Humpback Whale NMS (HIHWNMS) has four priority challenges, entanglement/marine debris-biological, large commercial vessel traffic, recreational vessel traffic, and marine mammal injury/harm and permits/takings. The site has a range of enforcement challenges, but all are seasonal and limited to fall, winter and spring, and none occur more than 50 times per year. Recreational vessel and large commercial traffic issues, marine mammal strandings and entanglement/marine debris incidents are the most prevalent, estimated at 10-50 times per year. A broad range of issues occur one to 10 times per year, including commercial fishing and gear violations, groundings, cruise ship incidents, overflight violations, ship strikes (marine mammals) and various issues associated with proximity to industrial development. The site shares boundaries with two National Wildlife Refuges areas (DOI) and two National Historical Sites (NPS, DOI). In addition two other National Historical Sites are in close proximity. The sanctuary is in State waters. There are 44 various zones/reserves or other protected areas in the sanctuary, some with different regulations than the rest of the site.

Papahānaumokuākea Marine National Monument. Enforcement in the Papahānaumokuākea Marine National Monument (PMNM) poses considerable logistical hurdles because of its remote location and size. Monument staff identified nine priority enforcement challenges. The only challenge estimated to happen more than 50 times per year is entanglement/marine debris-biological. In the 10 to 50 times per year category, are commercial fishing violations, anchoring incidents, underwater threats and significant storms. Up to 10 times per year the site estimates groundings, search and rescue support, fishing gear violations, and recreational vessel traffic, which is the only challenge with a seasonal component, as it does not take place in winter. All the challenges have a night use component. There are 12 reserve/marine protected area/zones encompassing over 115,000 square miles. NOAA, the U.S. Fish and Wildlife Service (DOI) and the State of Hawaii collectively manage the PMNM, as the co-trustees.

West Coast Region

Cordell Bank National Marine Sanctuary. This sanctuary is entirely in federal waters and many of the enforcement challenges are primarily related to the remote nature of the site. The site has three priority enforcement challenges, fishing/fishing gear violations, large commercial vessel traffic, and cruise ship discharges. While there are few enforcement challenges that are know to occur more than 10 times per year, the Cordell Bank NMS (CBNMS) potentially faces a wide range of occasional challenges, including those posed by recreational and large commercial vessel traffic, fishing and gear violations, ship strikes of marine mammals and other MMPA violations, illegal dumping/waste disposal, and mystery spills. Vessel search and rescue operations may occur in the site, as well as aircraft crashes due its proximity to major air corridors. The CBNMS faces no known seasonal or night use enforcement challenges. The sanctuary has no shared or contiguous jurisdiction with the state or the Department of the Interior, but shares its southern and eastern boundaries with the Gulf of the Farallones NMS. The site has 8 fishery management zones within it.

Channel Islands National Marine Sanctuary. The site has five priority challenges, traffic routing/anchoring incidents, spills of unknown origin, SPA or Zone, vessel groundings, and marine life disturbance by aircraft. The CINMS has several enforcement challenges that occur more than a few times a year. Commercial fishing and gear violations, and recreational vessel traffic incidents may occur more than 50 times a year, with both having night use components, and recreational vessels being seasonal only in the summer. Search and rescue mission support may occur 10 to 50 times per year, except in winter months. The site faces a wide variety of enforcement challenges from one to 10 times a year, including large commercial vessel incidents, cruise ships, mystery spills, groundings, aircraft crashes, ship strikes and mammal strandings, pipelines and oil/gas wells, and proximity to major port facilities and other shoreside industrial complexes. There are 12 reserves/protected areas/zones within the sanctuary, comprising 318 square miles. The CINMS has contiguous jurisdiction with DOI for the Channel Islands National Park.

Gulf of the Farallones National Marine Sanctuary. The site has four priority enforcement challenges, spills of unknown origin, large commercial vessel traffic, SPA or Zone, vessel groundings, and marine life disturbance by aircraft. Because of its proximity to a major metropolitan area and major harbor, the GFNMS has a long list of enforcement challenges that occur more than 50 times per year. These include large commercial and recreational vessel traffic, commercial fishing, mystery spills, search and rescue operations, groundings, anchoring incidents, marine mammal strandings, and waste site/dump issues. Most of these have seasonal components, for example, recreational vessel traffic is most prevalent in summer and fall, while mystery spills and groundings mostly occur in winter. Commercial fishing and search and rescue support also frequently have a nighttime component. In the frequency of 10 to 50 times per year are the enforcement challenges of overflight violations (spring and summer), fishing gear violations, outfalls (winter and spring when rains are heaviest) and zoning violations. From one to 10 times per year are a broad range of issues from ship strikes and entanglement (marine mammals), cruise ship incidents, water intake/desalination plants, to aircraft crashes, pipeline, and significant storm events.

The staff of the GFNMS also manages the northern section of Monterey Bay NMS. The sanctuary has contiguous jurisdiction with DOI. There are both offshore and nearshore areas, and 14 reserve/protected area/zones with different regulations than the rest of the site comprise less than 30 square miles.

Monterey Bay National Marine Sanctuary. The site has 12 priority enforcement challenges. The MBNMS has several enforcement challenges that may occur more than 50 times per year, these being recreational vessel/personal watercraft traffic, commercial fishing and gear violations, overflight violations, and marine mammal strandings. Both commercial fishing and fishing gear violations have a night use enforcement component. A number of enforcement challenges occur 10-50 times per year, most with night use, including large commercial vessel traffic, mystery spills, groundings, ship strikes and entanglements of marine mammals, outfalls, significant storms and zoning violations. Other enforcement challenges that occur one to 10 times per year, many at night-time, include cruise ships, anchoring incidents, search and rescue support, aircraft crashes, illegal salvage, dumping/waste sites, and underwater noise. The only enforcement challenge in MBNMS with a seasonal component is cruise ships, confined to spring and fall.

The MBNMS has identified 3,300 square miles as the area of significant concern for enforcement. There are 52 special reserve/protected areas/zones that have different regulations, comprising over 2,000 square miles of the sanctuary. The site includes both offshore and nearshore waters, and has contiguous jurisdiction with the US Forest Service, the Bureau of Land Management/DOI, as well as California State Parks. The northern portion of MBNMS is managed by the Gulf of the Farallones NMS.

Olympic Coast National Marine Sanctuary. The site has seven priority enforcement challenges. The Olympic Coast NMS has one category of enforcement challenges in which incidents occur more than 50 times per year – large commercial vessel traffic. Recreational vessel traffic incidents, as well as search and rescue, overflight violations and fishing and gear violations occur 10 to 50 times per year. A variety of challenges are estimated to occur one to 10 per year, including those associated with cruise ships, mystery spills, groundings, aircraft crashes, ship strikes and marine mammal strandings, entanglement and marine debris issues, and spoil disposal. The OCNMS faces several seasonal enforcement challenges -- recreational vessel incidents and overflight violations in the summer, and cruise ship incidents in both spring and summer. The sanctuary has a civil penalty schedule, but no summary settlement schedule. There are 3 National Wildlife Refuges in the sanctuary. The OCNMS has contiguous jurisdiction with the National Park Service/DOI, and includes traditional fishing areas for 4 coastal Indian tribes.

Southeast, Gulf of Mexico, and Caribbean Region

Flower Garden Banks National Marine Sanctuary. The site has four priority enforcement challenges, traffic routing/anchoring incidents, and spills of unknown origin, fishing/fishing gear violations, and recreational vessel traffic. Enforcement at the Flower Garden Banks National Marine Sanctuary is difficult, at best, given the sanctuary's remote location. The FGBNMS has three enforcement challenges in which incidents occur 10 to 50 times per year, including recreational vessel traffic, commercial fishing, and SAR missions. A large variety of enforcement challenges experience incidents one to 10 time per year, ranging from large commercial vessel traffic, lightering activities and mystery spills, anchoring incidents, and entanglement, to hurricanes, terrorism threats, and pipelines. Several challenges have seasonal components: for example, recreational vessel traffic and smuggling activities occur in all seasons except winter and hurricanes are prevalent in summer and fall only. All enforcement challenges have potential for night use. The site has a civil penalty schedule but no summary settlement schedule. The site has two JEAs, one with the State of Louisiana, and one with the State of Texas.

Florida Keys National Marine Sanctuary. The site has nine priority enforcement challenges. There are several enforcement challenges that occur more than 50 times per year: recreational vessel traffic, commercial fishing, cruise ships, SAR missions, groundings, anchoring, zoning violations, refugee/immigrant interdiction, smuggling/drug traffic, and proximity to transportation venues. Several categories of enforcement challenges have incidents that occur 10 to 50 times per year: large commercial vessel traffic, military traffic, fishing violations, illegal salvage ops, significant storms, and takings. A broad variety of enforcement challenges are estimated to occur between one to 10 times per year, including mystery spills, aircraft crashes, underwater threats, ship strikes, marine mammal strikes and strandings. There are seasonal components to several enforcement challenges: illegal salvage, hurricanes, and miscellaneous incidents are more prevalent in the summer and fall; while significant storms are more prevalent in winter and spring. Several activities have night challenges as well, including recreational and large commercial vessel traffic, commercial fishing, SAR missions, zoning violations, smuggling and refugee actions, military actions, storm events. The FKNMS has contiguous jurisdiction with National Park Service/DOI and overlapping jurisdiction with the United States Fish and Wildlife Service (DOI) and the State of Florida.

Grays Reef National Marine Sanctuary. The site has four priority enforcement challenges, fishing/fishing gear violations, traffic routing/anchoring incidents, entanglement/marine debris-biological, and marine mammal injury/harm and permits/takings. The GRNMS has two categories of enforcement challenges in which incidents occur 10-50 times per year, recreational vessel traffic and underwater threats. A variety of challenges are estimated to occur one to 10 times per year, including commercial fishing, large commercial vessel traffic, anchoring and fishing gear violations, ship strikes, entanglement, and storm events. GRNMS face several seasonal enforcement challenges, ship strikes and entanglement in the winter, and hurricanes in the summer and fall. There is no known nighttime use.

Northeast, Mid-Atlantic, and Great Lakes Region

MONITOR National Marine Sanctuary. The site has five priority enforcement challenges. The MONITOR NMS has no shoreline and only offshore waters, and has no contiguous or shared jurisdiction and no state waters. The site faces a range of enforcement challenges that are estimated to occur 10 to 50 times per year, including commercial fishing and gear violations and large commercial vessel impacts, anchoring incidents, entanglement/marine debris impact and illegal salvage/looting. Another set of issues that could divert enforcement assets less than 10 times per year include spills, storm events and possible seismic surveys or underwater noise. Enforcement at the MNMS is difficult given the sanctuary's remote location.

Stellwagen Bank National Marine Sanctuary. The site has six priority enforcement challenges. A two square mile area directly above the bank has been identified as the area of most concern for enforcement. Two enforcement challenges may occur more than 50 times per year; these are recreational vessel traffic (only in summer and fall) and vessel speed. Several challenges are likely from 10 to 50 times per year including commercial fishing violations, ship strikes and deepwater port (LNG) issues. A broader range of challenges may occur less than 10 times per year, including cruise ships (summer and fall seasons only), spills, support for search and rescue, entanglement/marine debris and dump site issues. Most challenges have a nighttime component. The SBNMS is situated entirely within federal waters and does not extend to a shoreline. There is one reserve/marine protected area within the sanctuary that is 147 square miles.

Thunder Bay National Marine Sanctuary. The site has four priority enforcement challenges, traffic routing/anchoring incidents, recreational vessel traffic, illegal salvage operations/looting, and entanglement/marine debris-maritime heritage. All the challenges in TBNMS have a seasonal aspect, since no activity occurs in winter. Only one enforcement challenge is estimated to occur more than 50 times per year and that is support for search and rescue missions. Those threats that occur 10 to 50 times per year include recreational vessel traffic, anchoring incidents, and illegal salvage/looting, which is a major issue for cultural resources. The TBNMS faces a longer list of potential challenges that occur from one to 10 times per year, including groundings, fishing gear violations, and entanglements that can directly impact the wrecks. Other challenges that may divert valuable enforcement resources include immigrant interdiction and smuggling. Several challenges have a night use element, like illegal salvage, recreational vessel traffic, and immigrant interdiction. The sanctuary has contiguous jurisdiction with the DOI, and is located entirely within State waters.

Appendix 2. Abbreviations

AIS: Automatic Identification System
AUS: Autonomous Unmanned Systems
CEA: Cooperative Enforcement Agreement
CEP: Cooperative Enforcement Program
ELINT: Electronic Intelligence
DEA: Drug Enforcement Administration
INS: Immigration and Naturalization Service
JEA: Joint Enforcement Agreement
FWCC: Fish and Wildlife Conservation Commission
MMPA: Marine Mammal Protection Act
NOAA: National Oceanic and Atmospheric Administration
NOS: National Ocean Service
NMFS: National Marine Fisheries Service
NMS: National Marine Sanctuary
NMSA: National Marine Sanctuaries Act
NMSS: National Marine Sanctuary System
OGC: Office of General Counsel
OLE: Office for Law Enforcement
ONMS: Office of National Marine Sanctuaries
PMNM: Papahānaumokuākea Marine National Monument
SPA: Sanctuary Preservation Area
UAS: Unmanned Aerial Systems
USCG: United States Coast Guard
USDOI: United States Department of the Interior
VMS: Vessel Monitoring System

Site Abbreviations
CI or CINMS: Channel Islands National Marine Sanctuary
CB or CBNMS: Cordell Bank National Marine Sanctuary
FB or FBNMS: Fagetele Nay National Marine Sanctuary
FG or FGBNMS: Flower Garden Banks National Marine Sanctuary
FK or FKNMS: Florida Keys National Marine Sanctuary
GF or GFNMS: Gulf of the Farallones National Marine Sanctuary
GR or GRNMS: Gray's Reef National Marine Sanctuary
HIHW or HIHWNMS: Hawaiian Islands Humpback Whale National Marine Sanctuary
M or MNMS: MONITOR National Marine Sanctuary
MB or MBNMS: Monterey Bay National Marine Sanctuary
OC or OCNMS: Olympic Coast National Marine Sanctuary
PMNM: Papahānaumokuākea Marine National Monument
SB or SBNMS: Stellwagen Bank National Marine Sanctuary
TB or TBNMS: Thunder Bay National Marine Sanctuary

Regions OLE & ONMS
NED: Northeast Division, OLE
SED: Southeast Division, OLE
SWD: Southwest Division, OLE
NWD: Northwest Division, OLE
PID: Pacific Islands Division, OLE
NE & GL: North East and Great Lakes Region, ONMS
SE & GOM: South East Atlantic, Gulf of Mexico and Caribbean Region, ONMS
WCR: West Coast Region, ONMS
PIR: Pacific Islands Region, ONMS

Appendix 3. Enforcement Functions

Function	Definition
Enforcement Planning and Analysis	The development of national, regional, and site enforcement plans, and includes identifying sanctuary resource threats, and developing enforcement profiles and priorities. Enforcement Planning and Analysis tools may include assessment of sanctuary use levels and patterns as well as violation trends, the cumulative review and assessment of data and reports from NOAA and non-NOAA sources, targeted surveys, field observations, empirical analyses, and literature reviews.
Enforcement Monitoring, Patrol, and Response	The field operational aspect of police and regulatory authority, enabling the implementation of enforcement plans, regulations to protect sanctuary resources. Enforcement monitoring and Patrol may include air /sea/land enforcement patrols and near real-time photoreconnaissance, remote sensing techniques, and video monitoring. The function is enhanced and augmented by public and volunteer observations and reporting. The goal is to implement 24/7/365 response capability, site-wide, and have the ability to respond to more than one simultaneous event.
Investigation and Injury Assessment	An in-depth follow-up effort after the initial response to an individual incident, and provides the link to case management and the legal mechanisms and processes, and where appropriate, to implementation of Section 312 of the NMSA. Investigation may include document and data reviews, evidence collection and preservation (chain of custody), personal interviews, and property seizures. Injury assessment is the bridge from enforcement to the damage assessment and restoration process. It takes place when an incident has resulted in injury to sanctuary natural or cultural resources, and involves measuring to objectively document the extent of injury and determine what restoration is preferable at the site.
Legal Mechanisms /Processes	The laws, regulations, and legal tools and procedures developed and applied to support sanctuary enforcement. They include regulatory promulgation, development of penalty and summary settlement schedules, individual case management and processing, prosecution and negotiation, and collection of fines.
Outreach and Education	The use of communication tools to deter sanctuary resource injury by achieving voluntary public compliance with, and support for, resource protection rules and regulations. The enforcement goals for outreach and education include, but are not limited to, regulatory compliance, increased public knowledge of activities that threaten the health of sanctuary resources, public reporting of observed violations, and a proactive public conservation ethic.
Management	The guidance, funding, coordination, and administrative support for a sanctuary enforcement program. It includes oversight of operational efforts including establishment of day-to-day priority setting. Management also entails coordinating interagency agreements and funding arrangements, fiscal planning, performance assessment, and management of collection accounts, staff allocation and training, and management of service and maintenance contracts.
Asset Requirements	Requirements may include acquisition and support of personnel, vehicles, vessels, aircraft, boat trailers, dive equipment, fuel, office space, boat docks, hangars, storage facilities, training facilities, office equipment, enforcement monitoring equipment, security equipment, regulatory buoys, outreach and education products, and maintenance services.

Appendix 4. USCG Living Marine Resource Asset Hours by District FY02-FY06.

		FY06			FY06
		Boat	Cutter	Aircraft	Total
District 1	SBNMS	2557.3	27751.7	1449.7	31758.7
District 5	MNMS	2805.1	13206	386	16397 1
District 7	FKNMS, GRNMS	1763.1	6905.8	122.7	8791.6
District 8	FGBNMS	1578.2	12586.3	475.9	14640.4
District 9	TBNMS	105.5	21.3	3.6	130.4
District 11	CINMS, MBNMS, GFNMS, CBNMS	510	6271.7	830.9	7612.5
District 13	OCNMS	397.2	5315.3	1134.1	6846.6
District 14	HIHWNMS, PMNM, FBNMS	349.4	1891.5	334.8	2575.7

		FY05			FY05
		Boat	Cutter	Aircraft	Total
District 1	SBNMS	2635.1	23551.6	1429.7	27616.4
District 5	MNMS	2403.3	11571.8	367	14342 2
District 7	FKNMS, GRNMS	1703.4	5574.2	108.7	7386.3
District 8	FGBNMS	1735.9	9091.7	702.6	11530.3
District 9	TBNMS	31	115.3	25.8	172.1
District 11	CINMS, MBNMS, GFNMS, CBNMS	464.4	7375.6	800.6	8640.5
District 13	OCNMS	659.4	5923.3	974	7556.8
District 14	HIHWNMS, PMNM, FBNMS	374.1	3720.3	359.9	4454.4

		FY04			FY04
		Boat	Cutter	Aircraft	Total
District 1	SBNMS	1618	16722.3	1254.3	19594.6
District 5	MNMS	1149.1	10053.1	299.9	11502.1
District 7	FKNMS, GRNMS	1058	3834.3	56.3	4948.5
District 8	FGBNMS	1455	7891.9	864.7	10211.5
District 9	TBNMS	0	0	29.7	29.7
District 11	CINMS, MBNMS, GFNMS, CBNMS	404.5	7008.1	698.4	8111
District 13	OCNMS	465.8	8110.7	881.6	9458.1
District 14	HIHWNMS, PMNM, FBNMS	144.3	3864.7	379.4	4388.4

		FY03			FY03
		Aircraft	Boat	Cutter	Total
District 1	SBNMS	1664.7	14477.2	917.2	17059 2
District 5	MNMS	534.3	7725.8	314.5	8574.5
District 7	FKNMS, GRNMS	976.6	6403.3	241.7	7621.6
District 8	FGBNMS	1608.1	4688.8	575.1	6872
District 9	TBNMS	0	14.3	73.5	87.8
District 11	CINMS, MBNMS, GFNMS, CBNMS	414.6	7982.2	571.4	8968.2
District 13	OCNMS	403.9	9160.4	775	10339 3
District 14	HIHWNMS, PMNM, FBNMS	170.7	2568.9	478.4	3218

		FY02			FY02
		Boat	Cutter	Aircraft	Total
District 1	SBNMS	1619	8570.9	840.6	11030.5
District 5	MNMS	332	7221.5	235.6	7789.1
District 7	FKNMS, GRNMS	1050.2	6015.7	293.9	7359.8
District 8	FGBNMS	2275	4484.3	332.8	7092.1
District 9	TBNMS	73.9	26	62	162
District 11	CINMS, MBNMS, GFNMS, CBNMS	178.2	3024.1	634.1	3836.4
District 13	OCNMS	621.5	5614	467.9	6703.4
District 14	HIHWNMS, PMNM, FBNMS	212.8	4704.2	655.3	5572.3

Source: U.S. Coast Guard Abstract of Operations database (as of 12 Aug 2007 update)
Note: The hours are listed by district and include all patrols where domestic living marine resources was a primary mission, which includes domestic fisheries, marine protected species, and marine sanctuaries. It does not, however, reflect resource hours where marine sanctuaries was a secondary or tertiary mission. As the information is listed by district is provides only a rough estimate for the amount of USCG presence within the NMS or Monument.

ENFORCEMENT ASSUMPTIONS MATRIX
FAGATELE BAY NATIONAL MARINE SANCTUARY

SECTION 1.

SURVEILLANCE, PATROL AND RESPONSE

Enforcement Challenges	Frequency of Enforcement Related Challenges *(Initial # from 2002 Resource Threats Survey)*				Temporal Complexity						Subtotal	Subtotal/category
	0 per year	1 to 10 x per year	10 to 50 x per year	>50 x per year	Winter	Spring	Summer	Fall	Significant Night Use	# of Special Events		
	0 points	2 points	5 points	10 points	Y/N	Y/N	Y/N	Y/N	Y/N	Actual #		
VESSEL BASED												**8**
Recreational Vessel Traffic		2			Y	Y	Y	Y	N			
Commercial Fishing		2			Y	Y	Y	Y	Y		2	
Large Commercial Vessel Traffic	0										0	
Military Traffic	0										0	
Cruise Ships	0										0	
Lightering Zones/Activities	0										0	
Mystery Spills (no responsible party and/or	0										0	
SAR Mission Support		2			Y	Y	Y	Y	Y		2	
Groundings		2			Y	Y	Y	Y	N		2	
Anchoring Incidents		2			Y	Y	Y	Y	N		2	
Aircraft crashes (proximity to air corridors)	0										0	
Overflight Violations	0										0	
U/W Threats	0										0	
Misc. (Seismic Surveys, U/W Noise)	0										0	
											0	
BIOLOGICAL & CULTURAL RESOURCES											0	**2**
Fishing/Fishing Gear Violations		2			Y	Y	Y	Y	Y			
Ship Strikes (marine mammals)	0										0	
Marine Mammal Strandings	0										0	
Entanglement/ Marine debris (incident/storm)		2			Y	Y	Y	Y	Y		2	
Illegal salvage operations/looting	0										0	
											0	
											0	
SHORELINE & INFRASTRUCTURE											0	**0**
Pipelines	0											
Oil/Gas Wells	0										0	
Outfalls	0										0	
Water Intakes/Desalination Plants	0										0	
Proximity to Interstate/Major Road/Rail Lines	0										0	
Power Plants	0										0	
Dump/Waste Sites	0										0	
Dredge Spoil	0										0	
Major Port Facilities	0										0	
Shoreside Industrial Complexes	0										0	
											0	
NATURAL DISASTERS											0	**6**
Earthquake		2			Y	Y	Y	Y	Y			
Tsunami		2			Y	Y	Y	Y	Y		2	
Hurricanes		2			N	N	Y	Y	Y		2	
Significant Storm Events		2			Y	Y	Y	Y	Y		2	
											0	
PERMITS											0	**0**
Zoning Violations	0											
"Takings"	0										0	
											0	
"SPECIAL" ISSUES											0	**0**
Refugee/Immigrant Interdiction	0											
Smuggling/Drug Traffic	0										0	
											0	

SECTION 2.

SURVEILLANCE, PATROL AND RESPONSE

Jurisdictional Complexity		Diversity				Geographic Coverage							
Shared or Contigous Jurisdiction with DO	Special ssues (Drugs mmigrant nterdiction)	< 5 User Groups	> 5 User Groups	Sig Heritage Resources	# T & E Species	Offshore	Nearshore	Offshore & Nearshore	Area of NMS (square miles)	Miles of Shoreline	Area of Significant concern *(if less than total area)*	# of Reserves/MPAs/Zones	Area of Reserve/MPA/Zones (square miles)
Y/N	Y/N	Y/N	Y/N	Y/N	Actual	Y/N	Y/N	Y/N	Actual	Actual	Actual	Actual	Actual
N	N	Y	N	N	1	N	Y	N	0.3	2.0	0.3	2	0.3

SECTION 3.

LOGISTICAL SUPPORT

Logistical Complexity			VESSEL BASED	BIOLOGICAL & CULTURAL RESOURCES	SHORELINE & INFRASTRUCTURE	NATURAL DISASTERS	PERMITS	"SPECIAL" ISSUES
Subtotal from Challenges			**18**	**2**	**6**	**2**	**0**	**0**
Infractions/Incidents occur in remote areas		Y/N	Y	Y	Y	Y	Y	Y
Enforcement requires multi-day vessel support		Y/N	N	N	N	N	N	N
# of Days per average mission		# of Days	1	1	1	1	1	1
Enforcement could require aerial or remote surveliance		Y/N	Y	Y	Y	Y	Y	Y

SECTION 4.

INFORMATION FROM PREVIOUS REQUIREMENTS STUDIES (For Reference Purposes)

			2005-2010				2010-2015	Vessel Type				
Small Boats Rqmts 2006-2015 (Days at Sea)			**DAS/Yr Need**				**DAS/Yr Need**	**I**	**II**	**III**		
(Type II Vessel-30-49 ft w/ limited			5				5	1				
			2006	**2007**	**2008**	**2009**	**2010**	**2011**	**2012**	**2013**	**2014**	**2015**
Aircraft Needs Assessment			0	0	0	0	0	0	0	0	0	0
# of Staff w/flight Clearance (NMS)			0	0								
# of Staff w/flight Clearance (OLE)												

SECTION 5.

ENFORCEMENT ACTION HISTORY

		2004	2005	2006	2007
# of Verbal Warnings					
# of Written Warnings					
# of Summary Settlements (NMSA			1		
# of Civil Penaltys (NMSA Sec. 307)					
# of ATBA violations (NMSA Sec. 307)					
# of NMSA permit violations (NMSA					
# of Natural Resource Damage					
# of Lacey Act violations					
# of MMPA violations					
# of ESA violations					
# of Magnuson violations					
# of OPA violations					
# of CWA violations					

FAGATELE BAY THREAT ASSESSMENT

			SEASONS					Prioritization (20 pts total)	Nearshore (0-12nm)	Offshore (12+ nm)	Prioritization (20 pts total)	Nearshore (0-12nm)	Offshore (12+ nm)
			W	S	S	F	N		100%			100%	
Approximate Frequency	1 to 10 per year	Recreational Vessel									2	100	
		Commercial Fishing									2	100	
		SAR Mission Support										100	
		Groundings									1	100	
		Anchoring Incidents									1	100	
		Fishing/Fishing Gear Vi lati ns						13	100		12	100	
		Entanglement/ Marine debris (incident/storm)						4	100		2	100	
		Earthquake											
		Tsunami											
		Hurricanes						3	100				
		Significant Storm Events											

ENFORCEMENT ASSUMPTIONS MATRIX

HAWAIIAN ISLANDS HUMPBACK WHALE NATIONAL MARINE SANCTUARY

SECTION 1.

SURVEILLANCE, PATROL AND RESPONSE

Enforcement Challenges	Frequency of Enforcement Related Challenges *(Initial # from 2002 Resource Threats Survey)*				Temporal Complexity						Subtotal	Subtotal/category
	0 per year	1 to 10 x per year	10 to 50 x per year	>50 x per year	Winter	Spring	Summer	Fall	Significant Night Use	# of Special Events		
	0 points	2 points	5 points	10 points	Y/N	Y/N	Y/N	Y/N	Y/N	Actual #		
VESSEL BASED												**29**
Recreational Vessel Traffic			5		Y	Y		Y			5	
Commercial Fishing		2			Y	Y		Y			2	
Large Commercial Vessel Traffic			5		Y	Y		Y			5	
Military Traffic			5		Y	Y		Y			5	
Cruise Ships		2			Y	Y		Y			2	
Lightering Zones/Activities	0										0	
Mystery Spills (no responsible party	0										0	
SAR Mission Support	0										0	
Groundings		2			Y	Y		Y			2	
Anchoring Incidents		2			Y	Y		Y			2	
Aircraft crashes (proximity to air	0										0	
Overflight Violations		2			Y	Y		Y			2	
U/W Threats		2			Y	Y		Y			2	
Misc. (Seismic Surveys, U/W Noise)		2			Y	Y		Y			2	
											0	
BIOLOGICAL & CULTURAL RESOURCES												**14**
Fishing/Fishing Gear Violations		2			Y	Y		Y			2	
Ship Strikes (marine mammals)		2			Y	Y		Y			2	
Marine Mammal Strandings			5		Y	Y		Y			5	
Entanglement/ Marine debris			5		Y	Y		Y			5	
Illegal salvage operations/looting	0										0	
											0	
											0	
SHORELINE & INFRASTRUCTURE												**14**
Pipelines	0										0	
Oil/Gas Wells	0										0	
Outfalls		2			Y	Y		Y			2	
Water Intakes/Desalination Plants		2			Y	Y		Y			2	
Proximity to Interstate/Major Road/Rail		2			Y	Y		Y			2	
Power Plants	0										0	
Dump/Waste Sites		2			Y	Y		Y			2	
Dredge Spoil		2			Y	Y		Y			2	
Major Port Facilities		2			Y	Y		Y			2	
Shoreside Industrial Complexes		2			Y	Y		Y			2	
											0	
NATURAL DISASTERS												**8**
Earthquake		2			Y	Y		Y			2	
Tsunami		2			Y	Y		Y			2	
Hurricanes		2			Y	Y		Y			2	
Significant Storm Events		2			Y	Y		Y			2	
											0	
PERMITS												**2**
Zoning Violations	0										0	
"Takings"		2			Y	Y		Y			2	
											0	
"SPECIAL" ISSUES												**4**
Refugee/Immigrant Interdiction		2			Y	Y		Y			2	
Smuggling/Drug Traffic		2			Y	Y		Y			2	
											0	

]

SECTION 2.

SURVEILLANCE, PATROL AND RESPONSE

Jurisdictional Complexity		Diversity				Geographic Coverage							
Shared or Contigous Jurisdiction with DO	Special ssues (Drugs mmigrant nterdiction)	< 5 User Groups	> 5 User Groups	Sig Heritage Resources	# T & E Species	Offshore	Nearshore	Offshore & Nearshore	Area of NMS (square miles)	Miles of Shoreline	Area of Significant concern *(if less than total area)*	# of Reserves/MPAs/Zones	Area of Reserve/MPA/Zones (square miles)
Y/N	Y/N	Y/N	Y/N	Y/N	Actual #	Y/N	Y/N	Y/N	Actual #	Actual #	Actual #	Actual #	Actual #
N	N	Y	N	Y	4	Y	Y	Y	1366	320		44	

SECTION 3.

LOGISTICAL SUPPORT

Logistical Complexity		VESSEL BASED	BIOLOGICAL & CULTURAL RESOURCES	SHORELINE & INFRASTRUCTURE	NATURAL DISASTERS	PERMITS	"SPECIAL" ISSUES
Subtotal from Challenges		**29**	**14**	**14**	**8**	**2**	**4**
Infractions/Incidents occur in remote areas	Y/N	Y	Y	N	Y	Y	N
Enforcement requires multi-day vessel support	Y/N	Y	Y	N	Y	Y	N
# of Days per average mission	# of Days	120					
Enforcement could require aerial or remote survelliance	Y/N	Y	Y	N	Y	Y	N

Total for all challenges

SECTION 4.

INFORMATION FROM PREVIOUS REQUIREMENTS STUDIES (For Reference Purposes)

		2005-2010				2010-2015	Number of Needs by NMSP Vessel Type				
Small Boats Rqmts 2006-2015 (Days at Sea)		**DAS/Yr Need**				**DAS/Yr Need**	**I**	**II**	**III**		
(Type II Vessel-30-49 ft w/ limited		120				120	4	1			
		2006	**2007**	**2008**	**2009**	**2010**	**2011**	**2012**	**2013**	**2014**	**2015**
Aircraft Needs Assessment		96	96	96	96	140	140	140	140	140	140
# of Staff w/flight Clearance		2	4	6							
# of Staff w/flight Clearance											
(1hr transit, 3 hrs, 2x/wk FW)											

SECTION 5.

ENFORCEMENT ACTION HISTORY

		2004	2005	2006	2007
# of Verbal Warnings					
# of Written Warnings					
# of Summary Settlements					
# of Civil Penaltys (NMSA Sec.					
# of ATBA violations (NMSA					
# of NMSA permit violations					
# of Natural Resource Damage					
# of Lacey Act violations					
# of MMPA violations					
# of ESA violations					
# of Magnuson violations					
# of OPA violations					
# of CWA violations					

HAWAIIAN ISLANDS HUMPBACK WHALE THREAT ASSESSMENT			Seasons					Prioritization (20 pts total)	Nearshore (0-12nm)	Offshore (12+ nm)	Prioritization (20 pts total)	Nearshore (0-12nm)	Offshore (12+ nm)
			W	S	S	F	N		100%			100%	
Approximate Frequency	10-50 per year	Recreational Vessel Traffic	x	x				4	100		6	100	
		Large Commercial Vessel Traffic	x	x				3	100		5	100	
		Military Traffic	..	..				3	100		3	100	
		Marine Mammal Strandings	x	x				4	100		4	100	
		Entanglement/ Marine debris incident/storm	x	x				6	100		2	100	
	1 to 10 per year	Commercial Fishing											
		Cruise Ships											
		Groundings											
		Anchoring Incidents											
		Overflight Violations											
		U/W Threats											
		Misc. Seismic Surve s, U/W Noise)											
		Violations											
		Shi Strikes marine											
		Outfalls											
		Water Intakes/Desalination Plants											
		Proximity to Interstate/Major Road/Rail											
		Dump/Waste Sites											
		Dredge Spoil											
		Major Port Facilities											
		Shoreside Industrial Complexes											
		Earthquake											
		Tsunami											
		Hurricanes											
		Significant Storm Events											
		"Takings"											
		Refugee/Immigrant											

Appendix 5: Site Surveys Enforcement Assumptions by Site 2/2007
Threat Assessments by Site 12/2007

ENFORCEMENT ASSUMPTIONS MATRIX
PAPAHANAUMOKUAKEA MARINE NATIONAL MONUMENT

SECTION 1.

SURVEILLANCE, PATROL AND RESPONSE

Enforcement Challenges	Frequency of Enforcement Related Challenges *(Initial # from 2002 Resource Threats Survey)*				Temporal Complexity						Subtotal	Subtotal/category
	0 per year	1 to 10 x per year	10 to 50 x per year	>50 x per year	Winter	Spring	Summer	Fall	Significant Night Use	# of Special Events		
	0 points	2 points	5 points	10 points	Y/N	Y/N	Y/N	Y/N	Y/N	Actual #		
VESSEL BASED												**21**
Recreational Vessel Traffic		2			n	y	y	y	y		2	
Commercial Fishing			5		y	y	y	y	y		5	
Large Commercial Vessel Traffic	0				y	y	y	y	y		0	
Military Traffic	0										0	
Cruise Ships						y	y	y			0	
Lightering Zones/Activities	0					y	y	y			0	
Mystery Spills (no responsible party					y	y	y	y	y		0	
SAR Mission Support		2			y	y	y	y	y		2	
Groundings		2			y	y	y	y	y		2	
Anchoring Incidents			5		y	y	y	y	y		5	
Aircraft crashes (proximity to air	0										0	
Overflight Violations	0										0	
U/W Threats			5								5	
Misc. (Seismic Surveys, U/W Noise)	0										0	
											0	
BIOLOGICAL & CULTURAL RESOURCES											0	**12**
Fishing/Fishing Gear Violations		2			y	y	y	y	y		2	
Ship Strikes (marine mammals)	0											
Marine Mammal Strandings	0										0	
Entanglement/ Marine debris				10	y	y	y	y	y		10	
Illegal salvage operations/looting	0										0	
											0	
											0	
SHORELINE & INFRASTRUCTURE												**0**
Pipelines	0										0	
Oil/Gas Wells	0											
Outfalls	0										0	
Water Intakes/Desalination Plants	0										0	
Proximity to Interstate/Major Road/Rail	0										0	
Power Plants	0										0	
Dump/Waste Sites	0										0	
Dredge Spoil	0										0	
Major Port Facilities	0										0	
Shoreside Industrial Complexes	0										0	
											0	
NATURAL DISASTERS												**9**
Earthquake		2									2	
Tsunami		2									2	
Hurricanes	0										0	
Significant Storm Events			5								5	
											0	
PERMITS											0	**0**
Zoning Violations	0										0	
"Takings"	0										0	
											0	
"SPECIAL" ISSUES											0	**0**
Refugee/Immigrant Interdiction												
Smuggling/Drug Traffic											0	
											0	

Appendix 5: Site Surveys Enforcement Assumptions by Site 2/2007
Threat Assessments by Site 12/2007

SECTION 2.

SURVEILLANCE, PATROL AND RESPONSE

Jurisdictional Complexity		Diversity				Geographic Coverage							
Shared or Contigous Jurisdiction with DOI	Special Issues (Drugs, Immigrant Interdiction)	< 5 User Groups	> 5 User Groups	Sig. Heritage Resources	# T & E Species	Offshore	Nearshore	Offshore & Nearshore	Area of NMS (square miles)	Miles of Shoreline	Area of Significant concern *(if less than total area)*	# of Reserves/MPAs/ Zones	Area of Reserve/MPA/Zones (square miles)
Y/N	Y/N	Y/N	Y/N	Y/N	Actual #	Y/N	Y/N	Y/N	Actual #	Actual #	Actual #	Actual #	Actual #
Y	N	N	Y	Y	23	Y	Y	Y	137,797			12	115,419

SECTION 3.

LOGISTICAL SUPPORT

Logistical Complexity			VESSEL BASED	BIOLOGICAL & CULTURAL RESOURCES	SHORELINE & INFRASTRUCTURE	NATURAL DISASTERS	PERMITS	"SPECIAL" ISSUES
Subtotal from Challenges			**21**	**12**	**0**	**9**	**0**	**0**
Infractions/Incidents occur in remote areas		Y/N	y	y		y		
Enforcement requires multi-day vessel support		Y/N	y	y	y	y	y	y
# of Days per average mission		# of Days	2					
Enforcement could require aerial or remote survelliance		Y/N	y	y	y	y	y	y

SECTION 4.

INFORMATION FROM PREVIOUS REQUIREMENTS STUDIES (For Reference Purposes)

			2005-2010				**2010-2015**	**Number of Needs by NMSP Vessel Type**				
Small Boats Rqmts 2006-2015 (Days at Sea)			**DAS/Yr Need**				**DAS/Yr Need**	**I**	**II**	**III**		
(Type II Vessel-30-49 ft w/ limited			30				50			1		
			2006	**2007**	**2008**	**2009**	**2010**	**2011**	**2012**	**2013**	**2014**	**2015**
Aircraft Needs Assessment Information (Flight Hours)			540	540	540	540	540	405	405	405	405	405
# of Staff w/flight Clearance (NMS)												
# of Staff w/flight Clearance (OLE)												
1.5 transit time, 12 hour flights (wklySSF, monthly W)												
Doesn't match w/ infrastructure assessment, patrol 1/month												

SECTION 5.

ENFORCEMENT ACTION HISTORY

			2004	**2005**	**2006**	**2007**
# of Verbal Warnings						
# of Written Warnings						1?
# of Summary Settlements (NMSA Sec.						
# of Civil Penaltys (NMSA Sec. 307)						1?
# of ATBA violations (NMSA Sec. 307)						
# of NMSA permit violations (NMSA						
# of Natural Resource Damage						
# of Lacey Act violations						
# of MMPA violations						
# of ESA violations						
# of Magnuson violations						2
# of OPA violations						
# of CWA violations						

PAPAHANAUMOKUAKEA THREAT ASSESSMENT			SEASONS					Prioritization (20 pts total)	Nearshore (0-12nm)	Offshore (12+ nm)
			W	S	S	F	N		100%	
Approximate Frequency	>50 per year	Entanglement/ Marine debris (incident/storm)						0		
	10-50 per year	Commercial Fishing						3	80	20
		Anchoring Incidents						1	100	0
		U/W Threats								
		Significant Storm Events								
	1 to 10 per year	Recreational Vessel Traffic						1	50	50
		SAR Mission Support						2	20	80
		Groundings						3	100	0
		Fishing/Fishing Gear Violations								
		Earthquake								
		Tsunami						1	100	0
		Mystery Spills						1	50	50
		Zoning Violations (VMS requirement)						2	100	0
		"Takings" (technical violations)						1	50	50
		"Pirate" fishing (unflagged vessels)						2	0	100
		Commercial Shipping						1	10	90
		Vessel Discharge						2	80	20

ENFORCEMENT ASSUMPTIONS MATRIX
CORDELL BANK NATIONAL MARINE SANCTUARY

SECTION 1.

SURVEILLANCE, PATROL AND RESPONSE

Enforcement Challenges	Frequency of Enforcement Related Challenges *(Initial # from 2002 Resource Threats Survey)*				Temporal Complexity						Subtotal	Subtotal/category
	0 per year	1 to 10 x per year	10 to 50 x per year	>50 x per year	Winter	Spring	Summer	Fall	Significant Night Use	# of Special Events		
	0 points	2 points	5 points	10 points	Y/N	Y/N	Y/N	Y/N	Y/N	Actual #		
VESSEL BASED												
Recreational Vessel Traffic		2										**26**
Commercial Fishing		2									2	
Large Commercial Vessel Traffic		2									2	
Military Traffic		2									2	
Cruise Ships		2									2	
Lightering Zones/Activities	0										2	
Mystery Spills (no responsible party and/or		2									0	
SAR Mission Support		2									2	
Groundings	0										2	
Anchoring Incidents	0										0	
Aircraft crashes (proximity to air corridors)		2									0	
Overflight Violations	0										2	
U/W Threats			5								0	
Misc. (Seismic Surveys, U/W Noise)			5								5	
											5	
BIOLOGICAL & CULTURAL RESOURCES											0	
Fishing/Fishing Gear Violations		2										**6**
Ship Strikes (marine mammals)		2									2	
Marine Mammal Strandings	0										2	
Entanglement/ Marine debris	0										0	
Illegal salvage operations/looting		2									0	
											2	
											0	
SHORELINE & INFRASTRUCTURE											0	
Pipelines	0											**2**
Oil/Gas Wells	0										0	
Outfalls	0										0	
Water Intakes/Desalination Plants	0										0	
Proximity to Interstate/Major Road/Rail	0										0	
Power Plants	0										0	
Dump/Waste Sites		2									0	
Dredge Spoil	0										2	
Major Port Facilities	0										0	
Shoreside Industrial Complexes	0										0	
											0	
NATURAL DISASTERS											0	
Earthquake		2										**6**
Tsunami		2									2	
Hurricanes	0										2	
Significant Storm Events		2									0	
											2	
PERMITS											0	
Zoning Violations	0											**0**
"Takings"	0										0	
											0	
"SPECIAL" ISSUES											0	
Refugee/Immigrant Interdiction		2										**4**
Smuggling/Drug Traffic		2									2	
											2	

SECTION 2.

SURVEILLANCE, PATROL AND RESPONSE

Jurisdictional Complexity		Diversity				Geographic Coverage							
Shared or Contigous Jurisdiction with DO	Special ssues (Drugs, mmigrant nterdiction)	< 5 User Groups	> 5 User Groups	Sig Heritage Resources	# T & E Species	Offshore	Nearshore	Offshore & Nearshore	Area of NMS (square miles)	Miles of Shoreline	Area of Significant concern *(if less than total area)*	# of Reserves/MPAs/Zones	Area of Reserve/MPA/Zones (square miles)
Y/N	Y/N	Y/N	Y/N	Y/N	Actual #	Y/N	Y/N	Y/N	Actual #	Actual #	Actual #	Actual #	Actual #
									529				

SECTION 3.

LOGISTICAL SUPPORT

Logistical Complexity		VESSEL BASED	BIOLOGICAL & CULTURAL RESOURCES	SHORELINE & NFRASTRUCTURE	NATURAL DISASTERS	PERMITS	SPECIAL" ISSUES
Subtotal from Challenges		26	6	2	6	0	4
Infractions/Incidents occur in remote areas	Y/N						
Enforcement requires multi-day vessel support	Y/N						
# of Days per average mission	# of Days						
Enforcement could require aerial or remote survelliance	Y/N						

SECTION 4.

INFORMATION FROM PREVIOUS REQUIREMENTS STUDIES (For Reference Purposes)

						Number of Needs by NMSP Vessel Type				
		2005-2010				2010-2015				
Small Boats Rqmts 2006-2015 (Days at Sea)		**DAS/Yr Need**				**DAS/Yr Need**	**I**	**II**	**III**	
(Type II Vessel-30-49 ft w/		0				20			1	
		2006	**2007**	**2008**	**2009**	**2010**	**2011**	**2012**	**2013**	**2014**	**2015**
Aircraft Needs Assessment		0	0	0	0	0	0	45	45	45	45
# of Staff w/flight Clearance		0									
# of Staff w/flight Clearance											

SECTION 5.

ENFORCEMENT ACTION HISTORY

		2004	2005	2006	2007
# of Verbal Warnings					
# of Written Warnings					
# of Summary Settlements					
# of Civil Penaltys (NMSA					
# of ATBA violations (NMSA					
# of NMSA permit violations					
# of Natural Resource					
# of Lacey Act violations					
# of MMPA violations					
# of ESA violations					
# of Magnuson violations					
# of OPA violations					
# of CWA violations					

CORDELL BANK THREAT ASSESSMENT								Prioritization (20 pts total)	Nearshore (0-12nm)	Offshore (12+ nm)
			SEASONS						100%	
			W	S	S	F	N			
Approximate Frequency	10-50 per	U/W Threats								
		Misc. Seismic Survey s, U/W								
	1 to 10 per year	Recreational Vessel Traffic								
		Commercial Fishing								
		Large Commercial Vessel Traffic						8		100
		Military Traffic								
		Cruise Ships						2		100
		Mystery Spills (no responsible party and/or unknown substances)								
		SAR Mission Support								
		Aircraft crashes (proximity to air corridors)								
		Fishing/Fishing Gear Violations						10		100
		hi trik s marin mammals								
		Ille al salva e o erations/lootin								
		Dump/Waste Sites								
		Earthquake								
		Tsunami								
		Significant Storm Events								
		Refu ee/Immi rant Interdiction								
		Smuggling/Drug Traffic								

ENFORCEMENT ASSUMPTIONS MATRIX
CHANNEL ISLANDS NATIONAL MARINE SANCTUARY

SECTION 1.

SURVEILLANCE, PATROL AND RESPONSE

Enforcement Challenges	Frequency of Enforcement Related Challenges *(Initial # from 2002 Resource Threats Survey)*				Temporal Complexity F34						Subtotal	Subtotal/category
	0 per year	1 to 10 x per year	10 to 50 x per year	>50 x per year	Winter	Spring	Summer	Fall	Significant Night Use	# of Special Events		
	0 points	2 points	5 points	10 points	Y/N	Y/N	Y/N	Y/N	Y/N	Actual #		
VESSEL BASED												**45**
Recreational Vessel Traffic				10			Y		Y		10	
Commercial Fishing				10	Y	Y	Y	Y	Y		10	
Large Commercial Vessel Traffic		2			Y	Y	Y	Y	Y		2	
Military Traffic		2			Y	Y	Y	Y	N		2	
Cruise Ships		2							N		2	
Lightering Zones/Activities		2							N		2	
Mystery Spills (no responsible party and/or		2			Y	Y	Y	Y	N		2	
SAR Mission Support			5			Y	Y	Y	N		5	
Groundings		2				Y	Y	Y	Y		2	
Anchoring Incidents	0								N		0	
Aircraft crashes (proximity to air corridors)		2							N		2	
Overflight Violations		2							N		2	
U/W Threats		2									2	
Misc. (Seismic Surveys, U/W Noise)		2							N		2	
											0	
BIOLOGICAL & CULTURAL RESOURCES												**20**
Fishing/Fishing Gear Violations		2		10	Y	Y	Y	Y			12	
Ship Strikes (marine mammals)		2									2	
Marine Mammal Strandings		2									2	
Entanglement/ Marine debris (incident/storm)		2									2	
Illegal salvage operations/looting		2									2	
											0	
											0	
SHORELINE & INFRASTRUCTURE												**8**
Pipelines		2									2	
Oil/Gas Wells		2									2	
Outfalls	0										0	
Water Intakes/Desalination Plants	0										0	
Proximity to Interstate/Major Road/Rail Lines		2									2	
Power Plants	0										0	
Dump/Waste Sites	0										0	
Dredge Spoil	0										0	
Major Port Facilities		2									2	
Shoreside Industrial Complexes		2									2	
											0	
NATURAL DISASTERS												**2**
Earthquake		2									2	
Tsunami	0										0	
Hurricanes	0										0	
Significant Storm Events		2									2	
											0	
PERMITS												**2**
Zoning Violations		2									2	
"Takings"		2									2	
											0	
"SPECIAL" ISSUES												**2**
Refugee/Immigrant Interdiction	0										0	
Smuggling/Drug Traffic		2									2	
											0	

SECTION 2.

SURVEILLANCE, PATROL AND RESPONSE

Jurisdictional Complexity		Diversity				Geographic Coverage							
Shared or Contigous Jurisdiction with DO	Special ssues (Drugs, mmigrant nterdiction)	< 5 User Groups	> 5 User Groups	Sig. Heritage Resources	# T & E Species	Offshore	Nearshore	Offshore & Nearshore	Area of NMS (square miles)	Miles of Shoreline	Area of Significant concern *(if less than total area)*	# of Reserves/MPAs/Zones	Area of Reserve/MPA/Zones (square miles)
Y/N	Y/N	Y/N	Y/N	Y/N	Actual #	Y/N	Y/N	Y/N	Actual #	Actual #	Actual #	Actual #	Actual #
Y	N	N	Y	Y	21*	Y	Y	Y	1474	173	14#	12	318

*incls State listed, #doesn't incl. MHR

SECTION 3.

LOGISTICAL SUPPORT

Logistical Complexity		VESSEL BASED	BIOLOGICAL & CULTURAL RESOURCES	SHORELINE & INFRASTRUCTURE	NATURAL DISASTERS	PERMITS	"SPECIAL" ISSUES
Subtotal from Challenges		**45**	**20**	**8**	**2**	**2**	**2**
Infractions/Incidents occur in remote areas		yes	yes	yes	yes		
Enforcement requires multi-day vessel support		yes	yes		yes		
# of Days per average mission		3	3				
Enforcement could require aerial or remote survelliance		yes	yes		yes	yes	

SECTION 4.

INFORMATION FROM PREVIOUS REQUIREMENTS STUDIES (For Reference Purposes)

		2005 2010				**2010 2015**	**Number of Needs by NMSP Vessel Type**				
Small Boats Rqmts 2006-2015 (Days at Sea)		**DAS/Yr Need**				**DAS/Yr Need**	**I**	**II**	**III**		
(Type II Vessel-30-49 ft w/ limited overnight capability) Includes CG, NPS, CDFG vessels		500				640	4	1	4		
		2006	**2007**	**2008**	**2009**	**2010**	**2011**	**2012**	**2013**	**2014**	**2015**
Aircraft Needs Assessment Information		100	150	180	180	180	180	180	180	180	180
# of Staff w/flight Clearance (NMS)		2	4	4	4	4	4	4	4	4	4
# of Staff w/flight Clearance (OLE)											
(1/2transit,5hr S2x,wkly SF,Wmonthly)											

Assumptions: CG/7Das/mo, NPS/20Das/mo, CDFG/12Das/mo, CINMS/1.5Das/mo

SECTION 5.

ENFORCEMENT ACTION HISTORY

		2004	**2005**	**2006**	**2007**
# of Verbal Warnings		100+	100+	100+	
# of Written Warnings					
# of Summary Settlements (NMSA Sec.		0	0	0	
# of Civil Penaltys (NMSA Sec. 307)		1	0	0	0
# of ATBA violations (NMSA Sec. 307					
# of NMSA permit violations (NMSA Sec. 307 or 312)		0	0	0	
# of Natural Resource Damage		0	0	0	
# of Lacey Act violations		0	0	0	
# of MMPA violations		0	0	0	
# of ESA violations		0	0	0	
# of Magnuson violations		?	?	?	
# of OPA violations		?	?	?	1*
# of CWA violations		2	1	1	

CHANNEL ISLANDS THREAT ASSESSMENT			SEASONS					Prioritization (20 pts total)	Nearshore (0-12nm)	Offshore (12+ nm)
			W	S	S	F	N		100%	
Approximate Frequency	>50 per year	Fishing/Fishing Gear Violations *in MPAs*						* / 3		100
		Recreational Vessel Traffic						* / 3		100
		Commercial Fishing *in MPAs*						* / 3		100
		Zoning Violations in reserves						* / 3		100
		Zoning Violations (*primarily fishing violations)*						12*/0		
	10-50 per year	SAR Mission Support						2 / 1		100
	1 to 10 per year	Large Commercial Vessel Traffic								
		Military Traffic								
		Cruise Ships								
		Lightering Zones/Activities								
		Mystery Spills (no responsible party and/or unknown substances)						1 / 1		100
		Groundings						2 / 3		100
		Aircraft crashes (proximity to air corridors)								
		Overflight Violations								
		U/W Threats								
		Misc. (Seismic Surveys, U/W								
		Ship Strikes (marine mammals)						1/0		100
		Marine Mammal Strandings								
		Entanglement/ Marine debris incident/storm								
		Illegal salvage operations/looting								
		Pipelines								
		Oil/Gas Wells								
		Proximity to Interstate/Major Road/Rail Lines								
		Major Port Facilities								
		Shoreside Industrial Complexes								
		Earthquake								
		Significant Storm Events								
		"Takings"								
		Illegal discharges						0/ 3		100
		Smuggling/Drug Traffic								
		* included in Zoning Violations								

ENFORCEMENT ASSUMPTIONS MATRIX

GULF OF THE FARALLONES NATIONAL MARINE SANCTUARY

SECTION 1.

SURVEILLANCE, PATROL AND RESPONSE

Enforcement Challenges	Frequency of Enforcement Related Challenges *(Initial # from 2002 Resource Threats Survey)*				Temporal Complexity						Subtotal	Subtotal/category
	0 per year	1 to 10 x per year	10 to 50 x per year	>50 x per year	Winter	Spring	Summer	Fall	Significant Night Use	# of Special Events		
	0 points	2 points	5 points	10 points	Y/N	Y/N	Y/N	Y/N	Y/N	Actual #		
VESSEL BASED												**98**
Recreational Vessel Traffic				10			Y	Y		5 to 8	10	
Commercial Fishing				10	Y	Y	Y	Y	Y		10	
Large Commercial Vessel Traffic				10	Y	N	N	Y			10	
Military Traffic		2									2	
Cruise Ships		2									2	
Lightering Zones/Activities		2									2	
Mystery Spills (no responsible party and/or				10	Y						10	
SAR Mission Support				10	Y	Y	Y	Y	Y		10	
Groundings				10	Y						10	
Anchoring Incidents				10	Y	Y	Y	Y		2 to 5	10	
Aircraft crashes (proximity to air corridors)		2			Y	Y	Y	Y			2	
Overflight Violations			5			Y	Y				5	
U/W Threats				10	Y	Y	Y	Y			10	
Misc. (Seismic Surveys, U/W Noise)			5		Y	Y	Y	Y			5	
											0	
BIOLOGICAL & CULTURAL RESOURCES												**21**
Fishing/Fishing Gear Violations			5		Y	Y	Y				5	
Ship Strikes (marine mammals)		2				Y		Y			2	
Marine Mammal Strandings				10	Y	Y	Y	Y			10	
Entanglement/ Marine debris		2			Y	Y	Y				2	
Illegal salvage operations/looting		2						Y			2	
											0	
											0	
SHORELINE & INFRASTRUCTURE												**49**
Pipelines		2			Y	Y	Y	Y			2	
Oil/Gas Wells	0										0	
Outfalls			5		Y	Y					5	
Water Intakes/Desalination Plants		2									2	
Proximity to Interstate/Major Road/Rail				10	Y	Y					10	
Power Plants	0										0	
Dump/Waste Sites				10	Y	Y					10	
Dredge Spoil				10	Y	Y		Y			10	
Major Port Facilities				10	Y	Y	Y	Y			10	
Shoreside Industrial Complexes											0	
											0	
NATURAL DISASTERS												**5**
Earthquake		2			Y	Y	Y	Y			2	
Tsunami		1									1	
Hurricanes	0										0	
Significant Storm Events		2			Y	Y					2	
											0	
PERMITS												**7**
Zoning Violations			5		Y	Y	Y	Y			5	
"Takings"		2			Y	Y	Y	Y			2	
											0	
"SPECIAL" ISSUES												**4**
Refugee/Immigrant Interdiction		2									2	
Smuggling/Drug Traffic		2									2	
											0	

Appendix 5: Site Surveys Enforcement Assumptions by Site 2/2007
Threat Assessments by Site 12/2007

SECTION 2.

SURVEILLANCE, PATROL and RESPONSE

Jurisdictional Complexity		Diversity				Geographic Coverage							
Shared or Contigous Jurisdiction with DO	Special ssues (Drugs mmigrant nterdiction)	< 5 User Groups	> 5 User Groups	Sig Heritage Resources	# T & E Species	Offshore	Nearshore	Offshore & Nearshore	Area of NMS (square miles)	Miles of Shoreline	Area of Significant concern *(if less than total area)*	# of Reserves/MPAs/Zones	Area of Reserve/MPA/Zones (square miles)
Y/N	Y/N	Y/N	Y/N	Y/N	Actual #	Y/N	Y/N	Y/N	Actual #	Actual #	Actual #	Actual #	Actual #
Y	Y	N	Y	Y	25	Y	Y	Y	2400	72.4		14	<30

SECTION 3.

LOGISTICAL SUPPORT

Logistical Complexity		VESSEL BASED	BIOLOGICAL & CULTURAL RESOURCES	SHORELINE & INFRASTRUCTURE	NATURAL DISASTERS	PERMITS	"SPECIAL" ISSUES
Subtotal from Challenges		**98**	**21**	**49**	**5**	**7**	**4**
Infractions/Incidents occur in remote areas	Y/N	Y	Y	Y	Y	Y	N
Enforcement requires multi-day vessel support	Y/N	Y	N	N	N	N	
# of Days per average mission	# of Days	1	1	1	1	1	
Enforcement could require aerial or remote surveilliance	Y/N						

SECTION 4.

INFORMATION FROM PREVIOUS REQUIREMENTS STUDIES (For Reference Purposes)

		2005-2010				2010-2015	Number of Needs by NMSP Vessel Type				
Small Boats Rqmts 2006-2015 (Days at Sea)		**DAS/Yr Need**				**DAS/Yr Need**	**I**	**II**	**III**		
(Type II Vessel-30-49 ft w/ limited		120				120	1	1			
		2006	**2007**	**2008**	**2009**	**2010**	**2011**	**2012**	**2013**	**2014**	**2015**
Aircraft Needs Assessment		0	0	0	0	0	0	80	80	80.00	80
# of Staff w/flight Clearance (NMS)		0	4	4	4	5	5	5	5	5.00	5
# of Staff w/flight Clearance (OLE)											

SECTION 5.

ENFORCEMENT ACTION HISTORY

		2004	2005	2006	2007
# of Verbal Warnings			1	2	
# of Written Warnings			1	1	
# of Summary Settlements (NMSA				1	
# of Civil Penaltys (NMSA Sec.					
# of ATBA violations (NMSA Sec.					
# of NMSA permit violations					
# of Natural Resource Damage			1		
# of Lacey Act violations					
# of MMPA violations					
# of ESA violations					
# of Magnuson violations		3	6	6	
# of OPA violations					
# of CWA violations					

GULF OF THE FARALLONES THREAT ASSESSMENT		SEASONS					Prioritization (20 pts total)	Nearshore (0-12nm)	Offshore (12+ nm)
		W	S	S	F	N		100%	
Approximate Frequency: >50 per year	Recreational Vessel Traffic								
	Commercial Fishing								
	Large Commercial Vessel Traffic								
	Anchoring Incidents								
	Dump/Waste Sites								
	Dredge Spoil						3		100
	Major Port Facilities								
10-50 per year	Overflight Violations						5	80	20
	Misc. (Seismic Surveys, U/W								
	Fishing/Fishing Gear Violations								
	Outfalls								
	Zoning Violations						2	90	10
	U/W Threats								
	Marine Mammal Strandings								
	Proximity to Interstate/Major Road/Rail Lines								
	Cruise Ships								
1 to 10 per year	"Takings"								
	Aircraft crashes (proximity to air corridors)								
	Earthquake								
	Entanglement/ Marine debris (incident/storm)								
	Ille_al salva_e o_erations/lootin_								
	Lightering Zones/Activities								
	Military Traffic								
	Pipelines								
	Refugee/Immigrant Interdiction								
	Ship Strikes (marine mammals)								
	Significant Storm Events								
	Smuggling/Drug Traffic								
	Tsunami								
	Water Intakes/Desalination Plants								
	Mystery Spills (no responsible _art_ and/or unknown substances)						5	80	20
	SAR Mission Support								
	Groundings						5	80	20

ENFORCEMENT ASSUMPTIONS MATRIX
MONTEREY BAY NATIONAL MARINE SANCTUARY

SECTION 1.

SURVEILLANCE, PATROL AND RESPONSE

Enforcement Challenges	Frequency of Enforcement Related Challenges *(Initial # from 2002 Resource Threats Survey)*				Temporal Complexity						Subtotal	Subtotal/category	
	0 per year	1 to 10 x per year	10 to 50 x per year	>50 x per year	Winter	Spring	Summer	Fall	Significant Night Use	# of Special Events			
	0 points	2 points	5 points	10 points	Y/N	Y/N	Y/N	Y/N	Y/N	Actual #			
VESSEL BASED												**81**	Fireworks, Mavericks,
Recreational Vessel Traffic				10	Y	Y	Y	Y	N	12	22		Squid night fishing peaks
Commercial Fishing				10	Y	Y	Y	Y	Y		10		
Large Commercial Vessel Traffic			5		Y	Y	Y	Y	Y		5		
Military Traffic		2			Y	Y	Y	Y	Y		2		
Cruise Ships		2			N	Y	N	Y	Y		2		Mostly military & USCG
Lightering Zones/Activities		2			Y	Y	Y	Y	N		2		Many originate in harbors,
Mystery Spills (no responsible party			5		Y	Y	Y	Y	Y		5		Primarily Info support
SAR Mission Support		2			Y	Y	Y	Y	N		2		Peaks in spring & winter
Groundings			5		Y	Y	Y	Y	Y		5		Large anchors snagged
Anchoring Incidents		2			Y	Y	Y	Y	N		2		
Aircraft crashes (proximity to air		2			Y	Y	Y	Y	N		2		Peaks in clear weather
Overflight Violations				10	Y	Y	Y	Y	N	5	15		UXO, SS Montebello, MV
U/W Threats			5		Y	Y	Y	Y	N		5		UXO detonations,
Misc. (Seismic Surveys, U/W Noise)		2			Y	Y	Y	Y	N		2		MSDs, trash, anchors,
BIOLOGICAL & CULTURAL RESOURCES												**32**	
Fishing/Fishing Gear Violations				10	Y	Y	Y	Y	Y	2	10		Spec. Events - Commercial
Ship Strikes (marine mammals)			5		Y	Y	Y	Y	Y	1	5		Spec. Event - Rec Salmon
Marine Mammal Strandings				10	Y	Y	Y	Y	N		10		Peaks during summer/fall
Entanglement/ Marine debris			5		Y	Y	Y	Y	N		5		
Illegal salvage operations/looting		2			Y	Y	Y	Y	Y		2		
											0		
											0		
SHORELINE & INFRASTRUCTURE												**27**	
Pipelines/Cables		2			Y	Y	Y	Y	N		2		
Oil/Gas Wells	0				N	N	N	N	N		0		
Outfalls			5		Y	Y	Y	Y	Y		5		Storm water & sewage.
Water Intakes/Desalination Plants			5		Y	Y	Y	Y	Y		5		Power plant, aquarium,
Proximity to Interstate/Major Road/Rail			5		Y	Y	Y	Y	Y		5		Cliff vehicles, spills, train
Power Plants		2			Y	Y	Y	Y	Y		2		
Dump/Waste Sites		2			Y	Y	Y	Y	N		2		Military, SF12, SF14
Dredge Spoil		2			Y	Y	Y	Y	N		2		Peaks winter
Major Port Facilities		2			Y	Y	Y	Y	Y		2		
Shoreside Industrial Complexes		2			Y	Y	Y	Y	Y		2		Sand plant, cement plant,
											0		
NATURAL DISASTERS												**9**	
Earthquake		2			Y	Y	Y	Y	Y		2		
Tsunami		2			Y	Y	Y	Y	Y		2		
Hurricanes	0				N	N	N	N	N		0		
Significant Storm Events			5		Y	Y	Y	Y	Y		5		Peaks fall/winter
											0		
PERMITS												**5**	
Zoning Violations			5		Y	Y	Y	Y	N		5		
"Takings"											0		
											0		
"SPECIAL" ISSUES												**4**	
Refugee/Immigrant Interdiction		2			Y	Y	Y	Y	Y		2		
Smuggling/Drug Traffic		2			Y	Y	Y	Y	Y		2		
											0		

SECTION 2.

SURVEILLANCE, PATROL and RESPONSE

Jurisdictional Complexity		Diversity				Geographic Coverage							
Shared or Contigous Jurisdiction with DO	Special ssues (Drugs, mmigrant nterdiction)	< 5 User Groups	> 5 User Groups	Sig Heritage Resources	# T & E Species	Offshore	Nearshore	Offshore & Nearshore	Area of NMS (square miles)	Miles of Shoreline	Area of Significant concern (if less than total area)	# of Reserves/MPAs/Zones	Area of Reserve/MPA/Zones (square miles)
Y/N	Y/N	Y/N	Y/N	Y/N	Actual #	Y/N	Y/N	Y/N	Actual #	Actual #	Actual #	Actual #	Actual #
Y	Y	N	Y	Y	32	Y	Y	Y	5,319	268	3,300	52	2,009

Reserves include 22 MLPA areas, 9 state reserves, 11 MBNMS zones (including Davidson), GGNRA, Fitzgerald, Ricketts, CA Coastal Monument, and an estimated 6 future Federal MPAs

SECTION 3.

LOGISTICAL SUPPORT

Logistical Complexity		VESSEL BASED	BIOLOGICAL & CULTURAL RESOURCES	SHORELINE & INFRASTRUCTURE	NATURAL DISASTERS	PERMITS	"SPECIAL" ISSUES
Subtotal from Challenges		74	47	46	14	13	17
Infractions/Incidents occur in remote areas	Y/N	Y	Y	Y	Y	Y	Y
Enforcement requires multi-day vessel support	Y/N	Y	Y	N	N	N	N
# of Days per average mission	# of Days	1	2	1	1	1	1
Enforcement could require aerial or remote survelliance	Y/N	Y	Y	Y	Y	Y	Y

SECTION 4.

INFORMATION FROM PREVIOUS REQUIREMENTS STUDIES (For Reference Purposes)

		2005-2010	Number of Needs by NMSP Vessel Type			2010-2015	Number of Needs by NMSP Vessel Type						
Small Boats Rqmts 2006-2015 (Days at Sea)		DAS/Yr Need	I	II	III	DAS/Yr Need	I	II	III	Answers are w/o NMA Values reflect 100% dedicated enforcement vessels & enforcement boat operating hours			
(Type II Vessel-30-49 ft w/ limited overnight capability)		431	2	1		431	2	1					
				2006	**2007**	**2008**	**2009**	**2010**	**2011**	**2012**	**2013**	**2014**	**2015**
Aircraft Needs Assessment				44	44	88	100	100	200	288	288	288	288
# of Staff w/flight Clearance (NMS)				0	1	2	2	3	3	3	3	3	3
# of Staff w/flight Clearance (OLE)				0	1	1	2	2	2	3	3	3	3
(1/2 hrs 4hrs)													
Answers w/ NMA													

SECTION 5.

ENFORCEMENT ACTION HISTORY

		2004	2005	2006	2007
# of Verbal Warnings		34	28	25	10
# of Written Warnings		7	2	3	0
# of Summary Settlements (NMSA		5	3	0	0
# of Civil Penaltys (NMSA Sec.		4	3	0	
# of ATBA violations (NMSA Sec.		12	5	7	0
# of NMSA permit violations		0	2	2	0
# of Natural Resource Damage		1	2	0	0
# of Lacey Act violations		0	0	0	0
# of MMPA violations		11	6	10	5
# of ESA violations		3	4	2	1
# of Magnuson violations		N/A	N/A	N/A	N/A
# of OPA violations		4	2	2	2
# of CWA violations		0	2	0	0

#Did not incl. NMA

MONTERY BAY THREAT ASSE[illegible]		SEASONS					Prioritization (20 pts total)	Nearshore (0-12nm)	Offshore (12+ nm)	
								100%		
Approximate Frequency: >50 per year	Recreational Vessel Traffic						1	90	10	
	Commercial Fishing						1	70	30	
	Overflight Violations						1	100		
	Fishing/Fishing Gear Violations						2	70	30	*in future MPAs*
	Marine Mammal *harrassment/harm/injury*						2	100		
Approximate Frequency: 10-50 per year	Large Commercial Vessel Traffic						1	50	50	
	M_ster_ S_ills _no responsible _art_ and/or unknown substances)						1	80	20	
	Groundings						2	80	20	*to Big Sur & south*
	U/W Threats							100		
	Ship Strikes (marine mammals)							50	50	
	Entanglement/ Marine debris (incident/storm)						1	90	10	
	Outfalls						1	100		
	Water Intakes/Desalination Plants							100		
	Proximity to Interstate/Major Road/Rail Lines							100		
	Significant Storm Events						1	100		
	Zoning Violations						2	80	20	*in future MPAs*
Approximate Frequency: 1 to 10 per year	Military Traffic							50	50	
	Cruise Ships *ille_al vessel dischar_e*						1	80	20	
	Lightering Zones/Activities							100		
	SAR Mission Support						1	80	20	
	Anchoring Incide[illegible]						1	100		
	Aircraft crashes (proximity to air							50	50	
	Misc. (Seismic Surveys, U/W Noise)							50	50	
	Illegal salvage operations/looting							100		
	Pipelines/Cables							100		
	Power Plants							100		
	Dump/Waste Sites							100		
	Dredge Spoil							100		
	Major Port Facilities							100		
	Shoreside Industrial Complexes							100		
	Earthquake							100		
	Tsunami							100		
	Refu_ee/Immi_rant Interdiction							80	20	
	Smuggling/Drug Traffic							80	20	

ENFORCEMENT ASSUMPTIONS MATRIX
OLYMPIC COAST NATIONAL MARINE SANCTUARY

SECTION 1.

SURVEILLANCE, PATROL AND RESPONSE

Enforcement Challenges	Frequency of Enforcement Related Challenges *(Initial # from 2002 Resource Threats Survey)*				Temporal Complexity						Subtotal	Subtotal/category
	0 per year	1 to 10 x per year	10 to 50 x per year	>50 x per year	Winter	Spring	Summer	Fall	Significant Night Use	# of Special Events		
	0 points	2 points	5 points	10 points	Y/N	Y/N	Y/N	Y/N	Y/N	Actual #		
VESSEL BASED												**44**
Recreational Vessel Traffic			5				Y				5	
Commercial Fishing		2									2	
Large Commercial Vessel Traffic				10							10	
Military Traffic			5								5	
Cruise Ships		2				Y	Y				2	
Lightering Zones/Activities	0										0	
Mystery Spills (no responsible party and/or		2									2	
SAR Mission Support			5								5	
Groundings		2									2	
Anchoring Incidents	0										0	
Aircraft crashes (proximity to air corridors)		2									2	
Overflight Violations			5				Y				5	
U/W Threats		2									2	
Misc. (Seismic Surveys, U/W Noise)		2									2	
											0	
BIOLOGICAL & CULTURAL RESOURCES												**13**
Fishing/Fishing Gear Violations			5								5	
Ship Strikes (marine mammals)		2									2	
Marine Mammal Strandings		2									2	
Entanglement/ Marine debris (incident/storm)		2									2	
Illegal salvage operations/looting		2									2	
											0	
											0	
SHORELINE & INFRASTRUCTURE												**4**
Pipelines	0										0	
Oil/Gas Wells	0										0	
Outfalls	0										0	
Water Intakes/Desalination Plants	0										0	
Proximity to Interstate/Major Road/Rail Lines	0										0	
Power Plants		2									2	
Dump/Waste Sites	0										0	
Dredge Spoil		2									2	
Major Port Facilities	0										0	
Shoreside Industrial Complexes	0										0	
											0	
NATURAL DISASTERS												**6**
Earthquake		2									2	
Tsunami		2									2	
Hurricanes	0										0	
Significant Storm Events		2									2	
											0	
PERMITS												**4**
Zoning Violations		2									2	
"Takings"		2									2	
											0	
"SPECIAL" ISSUES												**4**
Refugee/Immigrant Interdiction	0										0	
Smuggling/Drug Traffic		2									2	
Coordination with Treaty Tribes management		2									2	

SECTION 2.

SURVEILLANCE, PATROL AND RESPONSE

Jurisdictional Complexity		Diversity				Geographic Coverage							
Shared or Contigous Jurisdiction with DO	Special ssues (Drugs, mmigrant nterdiction)	< 5 User Groups	> 5 User Groups	Sig Heritage Resources	# T & E Species	Offshore	Nearshore	Offshore & Nearshore	Area of NMS (square miles)	Miles of Shoreline	Area of Significant concern *(if less than total area)*	# of Reserves/MPAs/Zones	Area of Reserve/MPA/Zones (square miles)
Y/N	Y/N	Y/N	Y/N	Y/N	Actual #	Y/N	Y/N	Y/N	Actual #	Actual #	Actual #	Actual #	Actual #
Y	Y		Y	Y	17	Y	Y	Y	3189	121	8	3	211

SECTION 3.

LOGISTICAL SUPPORT

Logistical Complexity		VESSEL BASED	BIOLOGICAL & CULTURAL RESOURCES	SHORELINE & INFRASTRUCTURE	NATURAL DISASTERS	PERMITS	"SPECIAL" ISSUES
Subtotal from Challenges		**44**	**13**	**4**	**6**	**4**	**4**
Infractions/Incidents occur in remote areas	Y/N	Y	Y	N	Y	Y	Y
Enforcement requires multi-day vessel support	Y/N	Y	N	N	N	N	N
# of Days per average mission	# of Days	3	1	1	1	1	1
Enforcement could require aerial or remote surveillance	Y/N	Y	Y	N	Y	Y	Y

SECTION 4.

INFORMATION FROM PREVIOUS REQUIREMENTS STUDIES (For Reference Purposes)

		2005-2010				2010-2015	Number of Needs by NMSP Vessel Type				
Small Boats Rqmts 2006-2015 (Days at Sea)		**DAS/Yr Need**				**DAS/Yr Need**	**I**	**II**	**III**		
(Type II Vessel-30-49 ft w/ limited		10				40		2			
		2006	**2007**	**2008**	**2009**	**2010**	**2011**	**2012**	**2013**	**2014**	**2015**
Aircraft Needs Assessment		10	20	20	40	40	60	80	122.5	122.5	122.5
# of Staff w/flight Clearance (NMS)		0									
# of Staff w/flight Clearance (OLE)		2									

SECTION 5.

ENFORCEMENT ACTION HISTORY

		2004	2005	2006	2007
NMS violations investigated		4	5	2	
# of Verbal Warnings					
# of Written Warnings		3			
# of Summary Settlements (NMSA					
# of Civil Penaltys (NMSA Sec.		1			
# of ATBA violations (NMSA Sec. 307)		280	191	TBD	
# of NMSA permit violations				1	
# of Natural Resource Damage		0	0	0	
# of Lacey Act violations					
# of MMPA violations					
# of ESA violations					
# of Magnuson violations					
# of OPA violations			3		
# of CWA violations					

OLYMPIC COAST THREAT ASSESSMENT		SEASONS					Prioritization (20 pts total)	Nearshore (0-12nm)	Offshore (12+ nm)
Approximate Frequency		[illegible]	[illegible]	[illegible]	F	[illegible]		100%	
10-50 per year	Recreational Vessel Traffic								
10-50 per year	Military Traffic *Growing concerns about impacts of unregulated military operations.*						1	30	70
10-50 per year	SAR Mission Support								
10-50 per year	Overflight Violations						5	100	
10-50 per year	Fishing/Fishing Gear Violations						2	50	50
1 to 10 per year	Commercial Fishing								
1 to 10 per year	Cruise Ship/*Large Commercial Vessels Traffic/concern about spills, groundings, ATBA compliance*						8	20	80
1 to 10 per year	Mystery Spills (no responsible party and/or unknown substances)						2	70	30
1 to 10 per year	Groundings						1	100	
1 to 10 per year	Aircraft crashes (proximity to air								
1 to 10 per year	U/W Threats								
1 to 10 per year	Misc. (Seismic Surveys, U/W Noise)								
1 to 10 per year	Ship Strikes (marine mammals)								
1 to 10 per year	Marine Mammal Strandings								
1 to 10 per year	Entanglement/ Marine debris (incident/storm) *Greater marine debris/derelict fishing gear concern than*						1	100	
1 to 10 per year	Illegal salvage operations/looting								
1 to 10 per year	Power Plants								
1 to 10 per year	Dredge Spoil								
1 to 10 per year	Earthquake								
1 to 10 per year	Tsunami								
1 to 10 per year	Significant Storm Events								
1 to 10 per year	Zoning Violations *Zoning violations covered under overflight rating, ATBA zoning violations covered under large commercial vessels*								
1 to 10 per year	"Takings"								
1 to 10 per year	Smuggling/Drug Traffic								
1 to 10 per year	Coordination with Treaty Tribes management of their U&A's *Tribes manage activities within U&A, not NMSA*								

ENFORCEMENT ASSUMPTIONS MATRIX

FLOWER GARDEN BANKS NATIONAL MARINE SANCTUARY

SECTION 1.

SURVEILLANCE, PATROL AND RESPONSE

Enforcement Challenges	**Frequency of Enforcement Related Challenges** ***(Initial # from 2002 Resource Threats Survey)***				**Temporal Complexity**						**Subtotal**	**Subtotal/category**
	0 per year	1 to 10 x per year	10 to 50 x per year	>50 x per year	Winter	Spring	Summer	Fall	Significant Night Use	# of Special Events		
	0 points	2 points	5 points	10 points	Y/N	Y/N	Y/N	Y/N	Y/N	Actual #		
VESSEL BASED												**31**
Recreational Vessel Traffic			5		N	Y	Y	Y	Y		5	
Commercial Fishing			5		Y	Y	Y	Y	Y		5	
Large Commercial Vessel Traffic		2			Y	Y	Y	Y	Y		2	
Military Traffic		2			?	?	?	?	?		2	
Cruise Ships		2			?	?	?	?	?		2	
Lightering Zones/Activities		2			Y	Y	Y	Y	Y		2	
Mystery Spills (no responsible party and/or		2			Y	Y	Y	Y	Y		2	
SAR Mission Support			5		Y	Y	Y	Y	Y		5	
Groundings	0										0	
Anchoring Incidents		2			Y	Y	Y	Y	Y		2	
Aircraft crashes (proximity to air corridors)	0										0	
Overflight Violations	0										0	
U/W Threats		2									2	
Misc. (Seismic Surveys, U/W Noise)		2			Y	Y	Y	Y	Y		2	
											0	
BIOLOGICAL & CULTURAL RESOURCES												**8**
Fishing/Fishing Gear Violations		2			Y	Y	Y	Y	Y		2	
Ship Strikes (marine mammals)		2			?	?	?	?	?		2	
Marine Mammal Strandings	0										0	
Entanglement/ Marine debris (incident/storm)		2			Y	Y	Y	Y	Y		2	
Illegal salvage operations/looting		2			Y	Y	Y	Y	Y		2	
											0	
											0	
SHORELINE & INFRASTRUCTURE												**6**
Pipelines		2			Y	Y	Y	Y	Y		2	
Oil/Gas Wells		2			Y	Y	Y	Y	Y		2	
Outfalls	0										0	
Water Intakes/Desalination Plants	0										0	
Proximity to Interstate/Major Road/Rail Lines	0										0	
Power Plants	0										0	
Dump/Waste Sites		2			Y	Y	Y	Y	Y		2	
Dredge Spoil	0										0	
Major Port Facilities	0										0	
Shoreside Industrial Complexes	0										0	
											0	
NATURAL DISASTERS												**4**
Earthquake	0										0	
Tsunami	0										0	
Hurricanes		2			N	N	Y	Y	Y		2	
Significant Storm Events		2			Y	Y	Y	Y	Y		2	
											0	
PERMITS												**0**
Zoning Violations	0										0	
"Takings"	0										0	
											0	
"SPECIAL" ISSUES												**4**
Refugee/Immigrant Interdiction	0										0	
Smuggling/Drug Traffic		2			N	Y	Y	Y	Y		2	
Terrorism threat		2			Y	Y	Y	Y	Y		2	

SECTION 2.

SURVEILLANCE, PATROL AND RESPONSE

Jurisdictional Complexity		Diversity				Geographic Coverage							
Shared or Contigous Jurisdiction with DO	Special ssues (Drugs mmigrant nterdiction)	< 5 User Groups	> 5 User Groups	Sig Heritage Resources	# T & E Species	Offshore	Nearshore	Offshore & Nearshore	Area of NMS (square miles)	Miles of Shoreline	Area of Significant concern *(if less than total area)*	# of Reserves/MPAs/Zones	Area of Reserve/MPA/Zones (square miles)
					Actual				Actual	Actual	Actual	Actual	Actual
Y/N	Y/N	Y/N	Y/N	Y/N	#	Y/N	Y/N	Y/N	#	#	#	#	#
Y	Y	Y	N	N	3	Y	N	N	56	0	56	0	0

SECTION 3.

LOGISTICAL SUPPORT

Logistical Complexity			VESSEL BASED	BIOLOGICAL & CULTURAL RESOURCES	SHORELINE & INFRASTRUCTURE	NATURAL DISASTERS	PERMITS	"SPECIAL" ISSUES
Subtotal from Challenges			**31**	**8**	**6**	**4**	**0**	**4**
Infractions/Incidents occur in remote areas		Y/N	Y	Y	Y	Y		Y
Enforcement requires multi-day vessel support		Y/N	Y	Y	Y	Y		Y
# of Days per average mission		# of Days	3	3	5	5		3
Enforcement could require aerial or remote surveilliance		Y/N	Y	Y	Y	Y		Y

SECTION 4.

INFORMATION FROM PREVIOUS REQUIRMENTS STUDIES (For Reference Purposes)

			2005-2010				2010-2015	Number of Needs by NMSP Vessel Type				
Small Boats Rqmts 2006-2015 (Days at Sea)			**DAS/Yr Need**				**DAS/Yr Need**	**I**	**II**	**III**		
(Type II Vessel-30-49 ft w/ limited			42				89			4		
			2006	**2007**	**2008**	**2009**	**2010**	**2011**	**2012**	**2013**	**2014**	**2015**
Aircraft Needs Assessment			24	24	24	24	72	72	72	156	156	156
# of Staff w/flight Clearance (NMS)			4	4	4	5	5	5	5	6	6	6
# of Staff w/flight Clearance (OLE)			2	2	2	2	2	2	2	2	2	2

SECTION 5.

ENFORCEMENT ACTION HISTORY

		2004	2005	2006	2007
# of Verbal Warnings					
# of Written Warnings		0	0	0	0
# of Summary Settlements (NMSA		0	0	0	0
# of Civil Penaltys (NMSA Sec. 307)		0	0	0	0
# of ATBA violations (NMSA Sec. 307)					
# of NMSA permit violations (NMSA		0	0	0	0
# of Natural Resource Damage		0	0	0	0
# of Lacey Act violations					
# of MMPA violations					
# of ESA violations					
# of Magnuson violations					
# of OPA violations					
# of CWA violations					

FLOWER GARDEN BANKS THREAT ASSESSMENT								Prioritization (20 pts total)	Nearshore (0-12mm)	Offshore (12+ nm)
			SEASONS						100%	
			W	S	S	F	N			
Approximate Frequency	10-50 per year	Recreational Vessel Traffic								
		Commercial Fishing						3		100
		SAR Mission Support								
	1-10 per year	Large Commercial Vessel Traffic								
		Military Traffic								
		Cruise Ships								
		Lightering Zones/Activities								
		Mystery Spills (no responsible party and/or unknown substances)						1		100
		Anchoring Incidents						4		100
		U/W Threats						2		100
		Misc. (Seismic Surveys, U/W								
		Fishing/Fishing Gear Violations						3		100
		Ship Strikes (marine mammals)								
		Entanglement/ Marine debris (incident/storm)						1		100
		Illegal salvage operations/looting								
		Pipelines						1		100
		Oil/Gas Wells						4		100
		Dump/Waste Sites								
		Hurricanes						1		100
		Significant Storm Events								
		Smuggling/Drug Traffic								
		Terrorism threat								

ENFORCEMENT ASSUMPTIONS MATRIX

FLORIDA KEYS NATIONAL MARINE SANCTUARY

SECTION 1.

SURVEILLANCE, PATROL AND RESPONSE

Enforcement Challenges	Frequency of Enforcement Related Challenges *(Initial # from 2002 Resource Threats Survey)*				Temporal Complexity						Subtotal	Subtotal/category
	0 per year	1 to 10 x per year	10 to 50 x per year	>50 x per year	Winter	Spring	Summer	Fall	Significant Night Use	# of Special Events		
	0 points	2 points	5 points	10 points	Y/N	Y/N	Y/N	Y/N	Y/N	Actual #		
VESSEL BASED												**716**
Recreational Vessel Traffic				10	Y	Y	Y	Y	Y	25	35	
Commercial Fishing				10	Y	Y	Y	Y	Y	50	60	
Large Commercial Vessel Traffic			5		Y	Y	Y	Y	Y	50	55	
Military Traffic			5		Y	Y	Y	Y	Y	10	15	
Cruise Ships				10	Y	Y	Y	Y	N	96	106	
Lightering Zones/Activities	0				N	N	N	N	N	0	0	
Mystery Spills (no responsible party and/or		2			Y	Y	Y	Y	Y	10	12	
SAR Mission Support				10	Y	Y	Y	Y	Y	40	50	
Groundings				10	Y	Y	Y	Y	N	340	350	
Anchoring Incidents				10	Y	Y	Y	Y	N	10	20	
Aircraft crashes (proximity to air corridors)		2			Y	Y	Y	Y	Y	3	5	
Overflight Violations	0				N	N	N	N	N		0	
U/W Threats		2			N	N	N	N	N	2	4	
Misc. (Seismic Surveys, U/W Noise)		2			N	N	Y	Y	N	2	4	
BIOLOGICAL & CULTURAL RESOURCES												**892**
Fishing/Fishing Gear Violations			5		Y	Y	Y	Y	Y	833	838	#'s from Gov Report
Ship Strikes (marine mammals)		2			N	N	N	N	N	1	3	
Marine Mammal Strandings		2			N	N	N	N	N	2	4	
Entanglement/ Marine debris (incident/storm)		2			N	N	N	N	N	35	37	
Illegal salvage operations/looting			5		N	N	Y	Y	N	5	10	
SHORELINE & INFRASTRUCTURE												**84**
Pipelines		2			N	N	N	N	N	2	4	
Oil/Gas Wells	0				N	N	N	N	N	0	0	
Outfalls		2			N	N	N	N	N	5	7	
Water Intakes/Desalination Plants		2			N	N	N	N	N	2	4	
Proximity to Interstate/Major Road/Rail Lines				10	N	N	N	N	N	30	40	
Power Plants		2			N	N	N	N	N	2	4	
Dump/Waste Sites		2			N	N	N	N	N	3	5	
Dredge Spoil		2			N	N	N	N	N	2	4	
Major Port Facilities		2			N	N	N	N	N	2	4	
Shoreside Industrial Complexes		2			N	N	N	N	N	10	12	
NATURAL DISASTERS												**21**
Earthquake	0				N	N	N	N	N	0	0	
Tsunami	0				N	N	N	N	N	0	0	
Hurricanes		2			N	N	Y	Y	Y	10	12	
Significant Storm Events			5		Y	Y	N	N	Y	4	9	
											0	
PERMITS												**302**
Zoning Violations				10	Y	Y	Y	Y	Y	212	222	From Gov Report
"Takings"			5		Y	Y	Y	Y	Y	75	80	Baitfish permits
											0	
"SPECIAL" ISSUES												**536**
Refugee/Immigrant Interdiction				10	Y	Y	Y	Y	Y	466	476	
Smuggling/Drug Traffic				10	Y	Y	Y	Y	Y	50	60	
											0	

SECTION 2.

SURVEILLANCE, PATROL and RESPONSE

		Diversity				Geographic Coverage							
Shared or Contigous Jurisdiction with DO	Special ssues (Drugs mmigrant nterdiction)	< 5 User Groups	> 5 User Groups	Sig Heritage Resources	# T & E Species	Offshore	Nearshore	Offshore & Nearshore	Area of NMS (square miles)	Miles of Shoreline	Area of Significant concern *(if less than total area)*	# of Reserves/MPAs/Zones	Area of Reserve/MPA/Zones (square miles)
Y/N	Y/N	Y/N	Y/N	Y/N	Actual #	Y/N	Y/N	Y/N	Actual #	Actual #	Actual #	Actual #	Actual #
Y	Y	Y	Y	Y	115	Y	Y	Y	3840	1800	3840	70	1844

SECTION 3.

LOGISTICAL SUPPORT

Logistical Complexity		**VESSEL BASED**	**BIOLOGICAL & CULTURAL RESOURCES**	**SHORELINE & INFRASTRUCTURE**	**NATURAL DISASTERS**	**PERMITS**	**"SPECIAL" ISSUES**
Subtotal from Challenges		**716**	**892**	**84**	**21**	**302**	**536**
Infractions/Incidents occur in	Y/N	Y	Y	Y	Y	Y	Y
Enforcement requires multi-day	....						
# of Days per average mission	# of Days	3	0	0	10	0	0
Enforcement could require aerial	Y/N	Y	Y	Y	Y	Y	Y

SECTION 4.

INFORMATION FROM PREVIOUS REQUIREMENTS STUDIES (For Reference Purposes)

		2005-2010				**2010-2015**	**Number of Needs by NMSP Vessel Type**					
Small Boats Rqmts 2006-2015 (Days at Sea)		**DAS/Yr Need**				**DAS/Yr Need**	**I**	**II**	**III**			
(Type II Vessel-30-49 ft w/		1810				2375	0	36	2			
		2006	**2007**	**2008**	**2009**	**2010**	**2011**	**2012**	**2013**	**2014**	**2015**	
Aircraft Needs Assessment Information (Flight Hours)	102	89	48	136	136	136	136	136	136	136	136	FWC Pilot
# of Staff w/flight Clearance	0	0	2	4	6	8	8	8	8	8	8	
# of Staff w/flight Clearance	1	1										

SECTION 5.

ENFORCEMENT ACTION HISTORY

		200 .	**_005**	**2006**	**2007**
# of Verbal Warnings					
# of Written Warnings		2164	1851	0	
# of Summary Settlements		64	69	31	
# of Civil Penaltys (NMSA Sec.					
# of ATBA violations (NMSA		4	6		
# of NMSA permit violations					
# of Natural Resource Damage		32	41	23	
# of Lacey Act violations		1	1	1	
# of MMPA violations		0	0	0	
# of ESA violations		1	2	6	
# of Magnuson violations					
# of OPA violations					
# of CWA violations					
# of Complaints		**5787**	**8430**		
# of State Violations		**774**	**951**		
# of Disaster Hours		**1662**	**2575**		
# of Vessel Inspections		8136	8021	11258	

FLORIDA KEYS THREAT ASSESSMENT								Prioritization (20 pts total)	Nearshore (0-12nm)	Offshore (12+ nm)
			SEASONS						100%	
			W	S	S	F	N			
Approximate Frequency	>50 per yearr	Recreational Vessel Traffic						5	100	
		Commercial Fishing						2	100	
		Cruise Ships								
		SAR Mission Support								
		Groundings						6	100	
		Anchoring Incidents						1	90	10
		Proximit_ to Interstate/Ma_or Road/Rail Lines								
		Zoning Violations						2	100	
		Refugee/Immigrant Interdiction								
		Smuggling/Drug Traffic								
	10-50 per year	Large Commercial Vessel Traffic								
		Military Traffic								
		Fishin_/Fishin_ Gear Violations						1	100	
		Illegal salvage operations/looting						0		
		Significant Storm Events						1	100	
		"Takings"								
	1 to 10 per year	Mystery Spills (no responsible party and/or unknown substances)						0		
		Aircraft crashes (proximity to air corridors)						0		
		U/W Threats						0		
		Misc. (Seismic Surveys, U/W						0		
		Ship Strikes (marine mammals)						0		
		Marine Mammal Strandings						0		
		Entanglement/ Marine debris (incident/storm)						1	100	
		Pipelines						0		
		Outfalls						0		
		Water Intakes/Desalination Plants						0		
		P w r Plants						0		
		Dump/Waste Sites						0		
		Dredge Spoil						0		
		Major Port Facilities						0		
		Shoreside Industrial Complexes						0		
		Hurricanes						1		
		* 1 pt given to all items in category								

ENFORCEMENT ASSUMPTIONS MATRIX
GRAY'S REEF NATIONAL MARINE SANCTUARY

SECTION 1.

SURVEILLANCE, PATROL AND RESPONSE

Enforcement Challenges	Frequency of Enforcement Related Challenges *(Initial # from 2002 Resource Threats Survey)*				Temporal Complexity						Subtotal	Subtotal/category
	0 per year	1 to 10 x per year	10 to 50 x per year	>50 x per year	Winter	Spring	Summer	Fall	Significant Night Use	# of Special Events		
	0 points	2 points	5 points	10 points	Y/N	Y/N	Y/N	Y/N	Y/N	Actual #		
VESSEL BASED												**33**
Recreational Vessel Traffic			5		Y	Y	Y	Y	N	5	10	
Commercial Fishing		2			Y	Y	Y	Y	N	0	2	
Large Commercial Vessel Traffic		2			Y	Y	Y	Y	N	0	2	
Military Traffic	0				N	N	N	N	N	0	0	
Cruise Ships	0				N	N	N	N	N	0	0	
Lightering Zones/Activities	0				N	N	N	N	N	0	0	
Mystery Spills (no responsible party and/or	0				N	N	N	N	N	0	0	
SAR Mission Support		2			Y	Y	Y	Y	N	0	2	
Groundings	0				N	N	N	N	N	0	0	
Anchoring Incidents		2			Y	Y	Y	Y	N	5	7	
Aircraft crashes (proximity to air corridors)	0				N	N	N	N	N	0	0	
Overflight Violations	0				N	N	N	N	N	0	0	
U/W Threats			5		Y	Y	Y	Y	N	5	10	
Misc. (Seismic Surveys, U/W Noise)	0				N	N	N	N	N	0	0	
											0	
BIOLOGICAL & CULTURAL RESOURCES												**6**
Fishing/Fishing Gear Violations		2			Y	Y	Y	Y	N	0	2	
Ship Strikes (marine mammals)		2			Y	N	N	N	N	0	2	
Marine Mammal Strandings	0				N	N	N	N	N	0	0	
Entanglement/ Marine debris (incident/storm)		2			Y	N	N	N	N	0	2	
Illegal salvage operations/looting	0				N	N	N	N	N	0	0	
											0	
											0	
SHORELINE & INFRASTRUCTURE												**0**
Pipelines	0										0	
Oil/Gas Wells	0										0	
Outfalls	0										0	
Water Intakes/Desalination Plants	0										0	
Proximity to Interstate/Major Road/Rail Lines	0										0	
Power Plants	0										0	
Dump/Waste Sites	0										0	
Dredge Spoil	0										0	
Major Port Facilities	0										0	
Shoreside Industrial Complexes	0										0	
											0	
NATURAL DISASTERS												**4**
Earthquake	0										0	
Tsunami	0										0	
Hurricanes		2			N	N	Y	Y	N	0	2	
Significant Storm Events		2			Y	Y	Y	Y	N	0	2	
											0	
PERMITS												**2**
Zoning Violations	0										0	
"Takings"		2									2	
											0	
"SPECIAL" ISSUES												**0**
Refugee/Immigrant Interdiction	0										0	
Smuggling/Drug Traffic	0										0	
											0	

Appendix 5: Site Surveys Enforcement Assumptions by Site 2/2007
Threat Assessments by Site 12/2007

SECTION 2.

JURISDITIONAL COMPLEXITY

Jurisdictional Complexity		**Diversity**				**Geographic Coverage**							
SECT ON 2	Special ssues (Drugs, mmigrant nterdiction)	< 5 User Groups	> 5 User Groups	Sig Heritage Resources	# T & E Species	Offshore	Nearshore	Offshore & Nearshore	Area of NMS (square miles)	Miles of Shoreline	Area of Significant concern *(if less than total area)*	# of Reserves/MPAs/Zones	Area of Reserve/MPA/Zones (square miles)
Y/N	Y/N	Y/N	Y/N	Y/N	Actual #	Y/N	Y/N	Y/N	Actual #	Actual #	Actual #	Actual #	Actual #
N	N	Y	N	N	2	Y	N	N	22	0	5	0	

SECTION 3.

LOGISTICAL SUPPORT

Logistical Complexity		**VESSEL BASED**	**BIOLOGICAL & CULTURAL RESOURCES**	**SHORELINE & INFRASTRUCTURE**	**NATURAL DISASTERS**	**PERMITS**	**"SPECIAL" ISSUES**
Subtotal from Challenges		**12**	**4**	**0**	**2**	**0**	**0**
Infractions/Incidents occur in remote areas	Y/N	Y	Y	N	Y	Y	N
Enforcement requires multi-day vessel	Y/N	N	N	N	N	N	N
# of Days per average mission	# of Days	1	1	0	1	1	0
Enforcement could require aerial or remote	Y/N	Y	N	N	N	Y	N
# of Days/missions/yr		80				80	

SECTION 4.

INFORMATION FROM PREVIOUS REQUIREMENTS STUDIES (For Reference Purposes)

		2005-2010				2010-2015	Type				
Small Boats Rqmts 2006-2015 (Days at Sea)		DAS/Yr Need				DAS/Yr Need	I	II	III		
(Type II Vessel-30-49 ft w/ limited overnight capability)		80	-28		-37	90		3			
		2006	**2007**	**2008**	**2009**	**2010**	**2011**	**2012**	**2013**	**2014**	**2015**
Aircraft Needs Assessment Information (Flight Hours)		0	0	0	0	0	60	60	60	60	60
# of Staff w/flight Clearance (NMS)		0									
# of Staff w/flight Clearance (OLE)		0									

SECTION 5.

ENFORCEMENT ACTION HISTORY

		2004	**2005**	**2006**	**2007**
# of Verbal Warnings					
# of Written Warnings					
# of Summary Settlements (NMSA Sec.			1		
# of Civil Penaltys (NMSA Sec. 307)			1		
# of ATBA violations (NMSA Sec. 307)					
# of NMSA permit violations (NMSA Sec.					
# of Natural Resource Damage					
# of Lacey Act violations					
# of MMPA violations				1	
# of ESA violations					
# of Magnuson violations					
# of OPA violations					
# of CWA violations					

GRAY'S REEF THREAT ASSESSMENT								Prioritization (20 pts total)	Nearshore (0-12nm)	Offshore (12+ nm)
			SEASONS						100%	
			W	S	S	F	N			
Approximate Frequency	10-50 per	Recreational Vessel Traffic								
		U/W Threats								
	1 to 10 per year	Commercial Fishing								
		Large Commercial Vessel Traffic								
		SAR Mission Support								
		Anchoring Incidents						5		100
		Fishing/Fishing Gear Violations						7		100
		Ship Strikes (marine mammals)								
		Entanglement/ Marine debris (incident/storm)						5		100
		Hurricanes								
		Significant Storm Events								
		"Takings"						3		100

ENFORCEMENT ASSUMPTIONS MATRIX

MONITOR NATIONAL MARINE SANCTUARY

SECTION 1.

SURVEILLANCE, PATROL AND RESPONSE

Enforcement Challenges	Frequency of Enforcement Related Challenges (*Initial # from 2002 Resource Threats Survey*)				Temporal Complexity						Subtotal	Subtotal/category
	0 per year	1 to 10 x per year	10 to 50 x per year	>50 x per year	Winter	Spring	Summer	Fall	Significant Night Use	# of Special Events		
	0 points	2 points	5 points	10 points	Y/N	Y/N	Y/N	Y/N	Y/N	Actual #		
VESSEL BASED												**36**
Recreational Vessel Traffic			5		N	Y	Y	Y	N		5	
Commercial Fishing			5		Y	Y	Y	Y	Y		5	
Large Commercial Vessel Traffic			5		Y	Y	Y	Y	N		5	
Military Traffic	0	2			Y	Y	Y	Y	N		2	
Cruise Ships	0								N		0	
Lightering Zones/Activities	0								N		0	
Mystery Spills (no responsible party and/or unknown	0	2							N		2	
SAR Mission Support			5		Y	Y	Y	Y	N		5	
Groundings	0								N		0	
Anchoring Incidents			5			Y	Y	Y	N		5	
Aircraft crashes (proximity to air corridors)	0								N		0	
Overflight Violations	0								N		0	
U/W Threats			5		Y	Y	Y	Y	N		5	
Misc. (Seismic Surveys, U/W Noise)	0	2			Y	Y	Y	Y	N		2	
											0	
BIOLOGICAL & CULTURAL RESOURCES												**15**
Fishing/Fishing Gear Violations	0		5		Y	Y	Y	Y			5	
Ship Strikes (marine mammals)	0										0	
Marine Mammal Strandings	0										0	
Entanglement/ Marine debris (incident/storm)			5		Y	Y	Y	Y			5	
Illegal salvage operations/looting			5			Y	Y	Y			5	
											0	
											0	
SHORELINE & INFRASTRUCTURE												**0**
Pipelines	0										0	
Oil/Gas Wells	0										0	
Outfalls	0										0	
Water Intakes/Desalination Plants	0										0	
Proximity to Interstate/Major Road/Rail Lines	0										0	
Power Plants	0										0	
Dump/Waste Sites	0										0	
Dredge Spoil	0										0	
Major Port Facilities	0										0	
Shoreside Industrial Complexes	0										0	
											0	
NATURAL DISASTERS	0											**4**
Earthquake	0										0	
Tsunami	0										0	
Hurricanes	0	2				Y	Y	Y			2	
Significant Storm Events	0	2			Y	Y	Y	Y			2	
											0	
PERMITS												**2**
Zoning Violations	0										0	
"Takings"		2			Y	Y	Y	Y			2	
											0	
"SPECIAL" ISSUES												**2**
Refugee/Immigrant Interdiction	0										0	
Smuggling/Drug Traffic	0	2									2	

SECTION 2.

SURVEILLANCE, PATROL AND RESPONSE

Jurisdictional Complexity		Diversity				Geographic Coverage							
Jurisdictional Complexity	Special ssues (Drugs mmigrant nterdiction)	< 5 User Groups	> 5 User Groups	Sig Heritage Resources	# T & E Species	Offshore	Nearshore	Offshore & Nearshore	Area of NMS (square miles)	Miles of Shoreline	Area of Significant concern *(if less than total area)*	# of Reserves/MPAs/Zones	Area of Reserve/MPA/Zones (square miles)
Y/N	Y/N	Y/N	Y/N	Y/N	Actual # <5	Y/N	Y/N	Y/N	Actual #	Actual #	Actual #	Actual #	Actual #
N	N	N	Y	Y	Y	Y	N	N	1	0		1	1

SECTION 3.

LOGISTICAL SUPPORT

Logistical Complexity		VESSEL BASED	BIOLOGICAL & CULTURAL RESOURCES	SHORELINE & INFRASTRUCTURE	NATURAL DISASTERS	PERMITS	"SPECIAL" ISSUES
Subtotal from Challenges		**36**	**15**	**0**	**4**	**2**	**2**
Infractions/Incidents occur in remote areas	Y						
Enforcement requires multi-day vessel support	N						
# of Days per average mission	1	**1**	**14**			**7**	
Enforcement could require aerial or remote surveilliance	Y						

SECTION 4.

INFORMATION FROM PREVIOUS REQUIREMENTS STUDIES (For Reference Purposes)

		2005-2010				2010-2015	Number of Needs by NMSP Vessel Type			
Small Boats Rqmts 2006-2015 (Days at Sea)		**DAS/Yr Need**				**DAS/Yr Need**	**I**	**II**	**III**	
(Type II Vessel-30-49 ft w/ limited		36				144		1	1	
	2006	**2007**	**2008**	**2009**	**2010**	**2011**	**2012**	**2013**	**2014**	**2015**
Aircraft Needs Assessment	0	0	0	0	0	72	72	72	72	72
# of Staff w/flight Clearance	0	3	3	3	4	4	4	4	4	4
# of Staff w/flight Clearance	0	5	5	5	5	5	5	5	5	5

SECTION 5.

ENFORCEMENT ACTION HISTORY

		2004	2005	2006	2007
# of Verbal Warnings		0	0	0	0
# of Written Warnings		0	0	0	0
# of Summary Settlements		0	0	0	0
# of Civil Penaltys (NMSA Sec.		0	0	0	0
# of ATBA violations (NMSA		0	0	0	0
# of NMSA permit violations		0	0	0	0
# of Natural Resource Damage		0	0	0	0
# of Lacey Act violations		0	0	0	0
# of MMPA violations		0	0	0	0
# of ESA violations		0	0	0	0
# of Magnuson violations		0	0	0	0
# of OPA violations		0	0	0	0
# of CWA violations		0	0	0	0

MONITOR THREAT ASSESSMENT								Prioritization (20 pts total)	Nearshore (0-12nm)	Offshore (12+ nm)	Prioritization (20 pts total)	Nearshore (0-12nm)	Offshore (12+ nm)
			SEASONS										
			W	S	S	F	N		100%			100%	
Approximate Frequency	10-50 per year	Commercial Fishing						1		100	1		100
		Large Commercial Vessel Traffic											
		SAR Mission Support						0		100			
		Anchoring Incidents						3		100	3		100
		U/W Threats											
		Fishing/Fishing Gear Violations											
		Entanglement/ Marine debris (incident/storm)						3		100	2		100
		Illegal salvage operations/looting						10		100	10		100
	1 to 10 per year	Military Traffic											
		Mystery Spills (no responsible party and/or unknown substances)						2		100	2		100
		Misc. (Seismic Surveys, U/W											
		Hurricanes						1		100	2		100
		Significant Storm Events											
		"Takings"											
		Smuggling/Drug Traffic											

ENFORCEMENT ASSUMPTIONS MATRIX

STELLWAGEN BANK NATIONAL MARINE SANCTUARY

SECTION 1.

SURVEILLANCE, PATROL AND RESPONSE

Enforcement Challenges	Frequency of Enforcement Related Challenges *(Initial # from 2002 Resource Threats Survey)*				Temporal Complexity						Subtotal	Subtotal/category
	0 per year	1 to 10 x per year	10 to 50 x per year	>50 x per year	Winter	Spring	Summer	Fall	Significant Night Use	# of Special Events		
	0 points	2 points	5 points	10 points	Y/N	Y/N	Y/N	Y/N	Y/N	Actual #		
VESSEL BASED												**34**
Recreational Vessel Traffic				10*	N	N	Y	Y			0	
Commercial Fishing			5		Y	Y	Y	Y	Y		5	
Large Commercial Vessel Traffic			5		Y	Y	Y	Y	Y		5	
Military Traffic		2			Y	Y	Y	Y	Y		2	
Cruise Ships		2			N	N	Y	Y	Y		2	
Lightering Zones/Activities	0				N	N	N	N	N		0	
Mystery Spills (no responsible party		2			Y	Y	Y	Y			2	
SAR Mission Support		2			Y	Y	Y	Y	Y		2	
Groundings	0				N	N	N	N	N		0	
Anchoring Incidents	0						Y	Y			0	
Aircraft crashes (proximity to air		2			Y	Y	Y	Y	Y		2	
Overflight Violations	0					Y	Y	Y			0	
U/W Threats		2			Y	Y	Y	Y			2	
Misc. (Seismic Surveys, U/W Noise)		2			Y	Y	Y	Y	Y		2	
Vessel speed				10	Y	Y	Y	Y	Y		10	
BIOLOGICAL & CULTURAL												**9**
Fishing/Fishing Gear Violations		2			Y	Y	Y	Y	Y		2	
Ship Strikes (marine mammals)			5		Y	Y	Y	Y	Y		5	
Marine Mammal Strandings	0				N	N	N	N	N		0	
Entanglement/ Marine debris		2			Y	Y	Y	Y	Y		2	
Illegal salvage operations/looting	0					Y	Y	Y	Y		0	
											0	
											0	
SHORELINE & INFRASTRUCTURE												**7**
Pipelines	0										0	
Oil/Gas Wells	0										0	
Outfalls	0										0	
Water Intakes/Desalination Plants	0										0	
Proximity to Interstate/Major	0										0	
Power Plants	0										0	
Dump/Waste Sites		2			Y	Y	Y	Y	Y		2	
Dredge Spoil	0										0	
Major Port Facilities	0										0	
Shoreside Industrial Complexes	0										0	
Deepwater Ports (LNG)			5		Y	Y	Y	Y	Y		5	
NATURAL DISASTERS												**2**
Earthquake	0										0	
Tsunami	0										0	
Hurricanes	0										0	
Significant Storm Events		2			Y	Y	Y	Y	Y		2	
											0	
PERMITS												**2**
Zoning Violations	0										0	
"Takings"		2			Y	Y	Y	Y	Y		2	
											0	
"SPECIAL" ISSUES												**0**
Refugee/Immigrant Interdiction	0										0	
Smuggling/Drug Traffic	0										0	
											0	

* Assumption- fishing for striped bass in federal waters while likely become legal soon which will have enforcement

Appendix 5: Site Surveys Enforcement Assumptions by Site 2/2007
Threat Assessments by Site 12/2007

SECTION 2.

SURVEILLANCE, PATROL and RESPONSE

Jurisdictional Complexity		**Diversity**				**Geographic Coverage**							
Shared or Contigous Jurisdiction with DO	Special ssues (Drugs mmigrant nterdiction)	< 5 User Groups	> 5 User Groups	Sig Heritage Resources	# T & E Species	Offshore	Nearshore	Offshore & Nearshore	Area of NMS (square miles)	Miles of Shoreline	Area of Significant concern *(if less than total area)*	# of Reserves/MPAs/Zones	Area of Reserve/MPA/Zones (square miles)
Y/N	Y/N	Y/N	Y/N	Y/N	Actual #	Y/N	Y/N	Y/N	Actual #	Actual #	Actual #	Actual #	Actual #
N	Y		Y	Y	9	Y	N	N	846	0	2	1	174

SECTION 3.

LOGISTICAL SUPPORT

Logistical Complexity		**VESSEL BASED**	**BIOLOGICAL & CULTURAL RESOURCES**	**SHORELINE & NFRASTRUCTURE**	**NATURAL DISASTERS**	**PERMITS**	**"SPECIAL" ISSUES**
Subtotal from Challenges		34	9	7	2	2	0
Infractions/Incidents occur in remote areas	Y/N	N	N	N	N	N	N
Enforcement requires multi-day vessel support	Y/N	Y	N	N	N	N	N
# of Days per average mission	# of Days	1	2	1	1	1	1
Enforcement could require aerial or remote surveilliance	Y/N	Y	Y	Y	Y	N	Y

SECTION 4.

INFORMATION FROM PREVIOUS REQUIREMENTS STUDIES (For Reference Purposes)

		2005-2010				**2010-2015**	**Number of Needs by NMSP Vessel Type**				
Small Boats Rqmts 2006-2015 (Days at Sea)		**DAS/Yr Need**				**DAS/Yr Need**	**I**	**II**	**III**		
(Type II Vessel-30-49 ft w/ limited		250				250		2	2		
		2006	**2007**	**2008**	**2009**	**2010**	**2011**	**2012**	**2013**	**2014**	**2015**
Aircraft Needs Assessment		0	0	10	40	60	80	80	80	80	80
# of Staff w/flight Clearance		0		2	3	4	4	6	6	6	6
# of Staff w/flight Clearance											
(1/2hr, 1.5 hr)											

SECTION 5.

ENFORCEMENT ACTION HISTORY

		2004	**2005**	**2006**	**2007**
# of Verbal Warnings				25	
# of Written Warnings				12	
# of Summary Settlements				3	
# of Civil Penaltys (NMSA Sec.				3	
# of ATBA violations (NMSA					
# of NMSA permit violations					
# of Natural Resource Damage					
# of Lacey Act violations					
# of MMPA violations				3	
# of ESA violations				3	
# of Magnuson violations				8	
# of OPA violations					
# of CWA violations					

STELLWAGEN BANK THREAT ASSESSMENT			SEASONS					Prioritization (20 pts total)	Nearshore (0-12nm)	Offshore (12+ nm)
									100%	
Approximate Frequency	>50 per year	Vessel speed *roximit to whales*						5	50	50
		Commercial Fishing *(area, gear, species)*						6	50	50
	10-50 per year	Large Commercial Vessel Traffic *(noise, routing)*						1	50	50
		Shi Strikes marine mammals *(prosecution)*						0	50	50
		Deepwater Ports (LNG)						1		
	1 to 10 per year	Military Traffic								
		Cruise Ships								
		Mystery Spills (no responsible party and/or unknown substances) *Cruise Spills*						1	50	50
		SAR Mission Support								
		Aircraft crashes (proximity to air corridors)								
		U/W Threats								
		Misc. (U/W Noise)						1	50	50
		Fishin /Fishin Gear Violations								
		Entanglement/ Marine debris (incident/storm)						1	50	50
		Dump/Waste Sites						1	50	50
		Significant Storm Events								
		Maritime Heritage (looting)						3	50	50

ENFORCEMENT ASSUMPTIONS MATRIX

THUNDER BAY NATIONAL MARINE SANCTUARY

SECTION 1.

SURVEILLANCE, PATROL AND RESPONSE

Enforcement Challenges	Frequency of Enforcement Related Challenges *(Initial # from 2002 Resource Threats Survey)*				Temporal Complexity						Subtotal	Subtotal/category
	0 per year	1 to 10 x per year	10 to 50 x per year	>50 x per year	Winter	Spring	Summer	Fall	Significant Night Use	# of Special Events		
	0 points	2 points	5 points	10 points	Y/N	Y/N	Y/N	Y/N	Y/N	Actual #		
VESSEL BASED												**38**
Recreational Vessel Traffic			5		N	Y	Y	Y	Y	3	8	
Commercial Fishing		2			N	Y	Y	Y			2	
Large Commercial Vessel Traffic		2			N	Y	Y	Y	Y		2	
Military Traffic		2			N	Y	Y	Y	Y		2	
Cruise Ships	0				N	N	N	N	N		0	
Lightering Zones/Activities	0				N	N	N	N	N		0	
Mystery Spills (no responsible party and/or		2			N	Y	Y	Y	N		2	
SAR Mission Support				10	N	Y	Y	Y	N		10	
Groundings		2			N	Y	Y	Y	N		2	
Anchoring Incidents			5		N	Y	Y	Y	N		5	
Aircraft crashes (proximity to air corridors)	0				N	N	N	N	N		0	
Overflight Violations	0				N	N	N	N	N		0	
U/W Threats			5								5	
Misc. (Seismic Surveys, U/W Noise)	0				N	N	N	N	N		0	
											0	
BIOLOGICAL & CULTURAL RESOURCES												**9**
Fishing/Fishing Gear Violations		2			N	Y	Y	Y	N		2	
Ship Strikes (marine mammals)	0				N						0	
Marine Mammal Strandings	0				N						0	
Entanglement/ Marine debris (incident/storm)		2			N	Y	Y	Y	N		2	
Illegal salvage operations/looting			5		N	Y	Y	Y	Y		5	
											0	
											0	
SHORELINE & INFRASTRUCTURE												**10**
Pipelines	0										0	
Oil/Gas Wells	0										0	
Outfalls	0										0	
Water Intakes/Desalination Plants	0	2									2	
Proximity to Interstate/Major Road/Rail Lines		2									2	
Power Plants	0										0	
Dump/Waste Sites (Unexploded Ord. area is		2									2	
Dredge Spoil	0										0	
Major Port Facilities		2									2	
Shoreside Industrial Complexes		2									2	
											0	
NATURAL DISASTERS												**2**
Earthquake	0										0	
Tsunami	0										0	
Hurricanes	0										0	
Significant Storm Events		2									2	
											0	
PERMITS												**2**
Zoning Violations	0										0	
"Takings"		2			N	Y	Y	Y	Y		2	
											0	
"SPECIAL" ISSUES												**4**
Refugee/Immigrant Interdiction		2			N	Y	Y	Y	Y		2	
Smuggling/Drug Traffic		2			N	Y	Y	Y	Y		2	
Note: TB is on international boarder											0	

Appendix 5: Site Surveys Enforcement Assumptions by Site 2/2007
Threat Assessments by Site 12/2007

SECTION 2.

SURVEILLANCE, PATROL AND RESPONSE

Jurisdictional Complexity		Diversity				Geographic Coverage							
Shared or Contigous Jurisdiction with M-DNR	Special ssues (Drugs, mmigrant nterdiction)	< 5 User Groups	> 5 User Groups	Sig. Heritage Resources	# T & E Species	Offshore	Nearshore	Offshore & Nearshore	Area of NMS (square miles)	Miles of Shoreline	Area of Significant concern *(if less than total area)*	# of Reserves/MPAs/Zones	Area of Reserve/MPA/Zones (square miles)
Y/N	Y/N	Y/N	Y/N	Y/N	Actual #	Y/N	Y/N	Y/N	Actual #	Actual #	Actual #	Actual #	Actual #
y	Y		Y	Y		Y	Y	Y	448	76		0	0

* May increase to 3,800 plus square miles

SECTION 3.

LOGISTICAL SUPPORT

Logistical Complexity		VESSEL BASED	BIOLOGICAL & CULTURAL RESOURCES	SHORELINE & INFRASTRUCTURE	NATURAL DISASTERS	PERMITS	"SPECIAL" ISSUES
Subtotal from Challenges		38	9	10	2	2	4
Infractions/Incidents occur in remote areas	Y/N	Y	Y	N	Y	Y	Y
Enforcement requires multi-day vessel support	Y/N	Y	Y	N	N	N	Y
# of Days per average mission	# of Days	1	1*	1	1	1	1
Enforcement could require aerial or remote surveillance	Y/N	Y	Y	N	N	N	Y

*1 is ave , there is a need for occas multi days

SECTION 4.

INFORMATION FROM PREVIOUS REQUIREMENTS STUDIES (For Reference Purposes)

		2005-2010				2010-2015	Number of Needs by NMSP				
Small Boats Rqmts 2006-2015 (Days at Sea)		**DAS/Yr Need**				**DAS/Yr Need**	**I**	**II**	**III**		
(Type II Vessel-30-49 ft w/ limited		40				50		2		Include others	
USCG on water every day (April -Sept)											
		2006	**2007**	**2008**	**2009**	**2010**	**2011**	**2012**	**2013**	**2014**	**2015**
Aircraft Needs Assessment Information		0	0	0	0	0	0	0	0	0	0
# of Staff w/flight Clearance (NMS)		1	4	5	6	6	6	6	6	6	6
# of Staff w/flight Clearance (OLE)											

SECTION 5.

ENFORCEMENT ACTION HISTORY

		2004	2005	2006	2007
# of Verbal Warnings		0	0	0	
# of Written Warnings		0	0	0	
# of Summary Settlements (NMSA Sec.		0	0	0	
# of Civil Penaltys (NMSA Sec. 307)		0	0	0	
# of ATBA violations (NMSA Sec. 307)		0	0	0	
# of NMSA permit violations (NMSA		0	0	0	
# of Natural Resource Damage		0	0	0	
# of Lacey Act violations		0	0	0	
# of MMPA violations		0	0	0	
# of ESA violations		0	0	0	
# of Magnuson violations		0	0	0	
# of OPA violations		0	0	0	
# of CWA violations		0	0	0	

* USCG does +/ 70 boardings/yr, in addition to DNR and county

There are multiple state and USCG warnings/infractions

THUNDER BAY THREAT ASSESSMENT		SEASONS					Prioritization (20 pts	Nearshore (0-12nm)	Offshore (12+ nm)	Prioritization (20 pts total)	Nearshore (0-12nm)	Offshore (12+ nm)
		W	_	_	F	N		100%			100%	
Approximate Frequency												
>50 per year	SAR Mission Support						2	65	35	2	60	40
10-50 per year	Recreational Vessel Traffic											
	Anchoring Incidents						4	65	35	4	60	40
	U/W Threats											
	Illegal salvage operati ns/l tin_						14	55	45	14	60	40
1 to 10 per year	Commercial Fishing											
	Large Commercial Vessel Traffic											
	Military Traffic											
	Mystery Spills (no responsible _art_ and/or unknown substances)											
	Groundings											
	Fishing/Fishing Gear Violations											
	Entanglement/ Marine debris (incident/storm)											
	Water Intakes/Desalination Plants											
	Proximity to Interstate/Major Road/Rail Lines											
	Dump/Waste Sites (Unexploded Ord. area is a fire zone)											
	Major Port Facilities											
	Shoreside Industrial Complexes											
	Significant Storm Events											
	"Takings"											
	Refu_ee/Immi_rant Interdiction											
	Smuggling/Drug Traffic											

www.ingramcontent.com/pod-product-compliance
Lightning Source LLC
Chambersburg PA
CBHW081839170526
45167CB00007B/2846
* 9 7 8 1 4 9 6 0 2 5 8 9 0 *